CW00377147

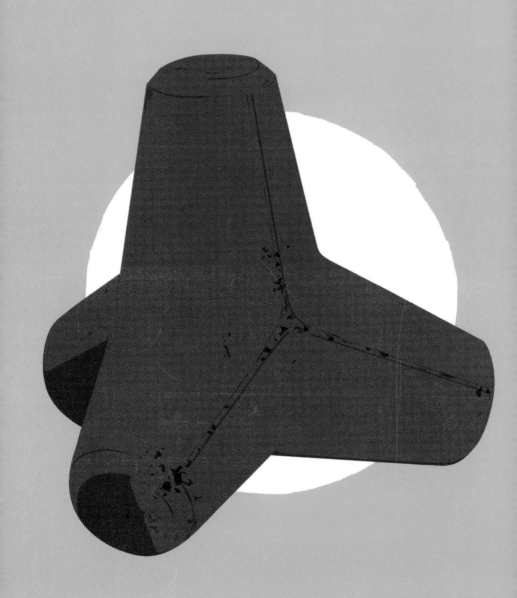

Wundor City Guide
Mumbai

मुंबई शहर
मार्गदर्शक

—

Edited by
Matthew Smith

First published in Great Britain in 2017 by Wundor Editions

Wundor Editions Ltd, 35B Fitzjohn's Avenue, London NW3 5JY

www.wundoreditions.com

Book Design and Art Direction – Matthew Smith

Design Assistant – Lauren Necati

Illustrator – Nikunj Patel

ISBN 978-0-9956541-4-3

Printed in Latvia by Livonia Print

WUNDOR

Editions

Guide to Mumbai

———

Edited by
Matthew Smith

"The city offers sanctuary by night, before becoming a vibrant colour palette of all life's hues by day. The sea gleams with hundreds of little suns reflecting off the tops of its modest waves, children run out of school pell-mell with their bright plastic slippers and their uniforms in disarray. Vendors move across the metropolis, making sure that all the cogs in this old machine are well-oiled, their saris and dhotis bright in the midday sun."

AMBARIN AFSAR
Writer

Navigation – p. 48

Contents
अनुक्रमणिका

———

Previous – Fort
Opposite – Bandra | Matthew Smith

· आगमन ·

Arrival

आगमन

Words and photos –
Matthew Smith

Dharavi

Kala Ghoda

Mumbai is populated by a number of animals. The same could be said for all cities. London's foxes have haunted street corners since the first wattle-and-daub-based tenements rose from the mud. Cockroaches and New Yorkers have a long-standing acquaintance. The possom works its way through the backyards of Sydney-siders and Portlandia-dwellers alike. But Mumbai is a city in which animals wander into the kingdom of men, and stay there. They do not skulk in the shadows. They don't recognise man as the ruler of an earthly paradise, fallen or no.

Dogs sprawl across pavements, track the wanderer on his journey, dart off, as though the visitor to the city were a guest of the canine kingdom, his journey incidental to those of its true denizens. Warthogs slumber peacefully in groups on piles of bio-refuse, beside swamps that border financial centres, with their tall buildings sporting international banking logos. And everywhere the wanderer goes, the crows are close at hand, whirling on the breeze, lifting and dropping off, loose shadows one moment, the next on a table nabbing something shiny with sharp beaks, before relaxing once more into the domain of the winds that sweep in over Mahim Bay, across Marine Drive and through the Gateway of India. The structures and byways of the city may have been made and named by men and women, but in Mumbai, creation must be shared by every creature, on two legs or four.

The final principality of the city, after those of the human and the animal, is that of the ocean, because Mumbai does not stop at the limits of its shores and its sea walls. The world beneath the waves has sustained it since its inception, and Mumbai is better surrounded than most, due to the fact that its hub regions reach out in the form of a narrow peninsula, so that this densely populated city parts the sea like the spears still used by the fishing communities. The city is well-protected from the ocean which rolls powerfully in stormy weather, and gleams the palest blue when calm under diamond-sunlight. But still, in a sense, the city itself is porous to its effects, because the residents welcome it into their lives, and rush to it loyally when the urge takes them. Visiting during monsoon season, this writer was reassured by his taxi driver, en route from the airport, that he had picked the best possible time of the year to come, as the rain grimaced at the window. I was led out of my confusion as a plan of action was proposed to me. I was to drop my suitcase off at the hotel, stroll through the voluminous rainfall – no umbrella would be required – and find my way to Chowpatty Beach, where I would find the rest of the city, having a raucous party. In particular, I was to find a good spot near the waves where I could be most thoroughly splashed, soaked and drenched. Then hit the barbecue.

I settled on that occasion for a dip in the hotel pool, under violet and midnight blue skies, as palm trees whipped around over my head, and the omnipresent crows rode the vortex of air created by the surrounding buildings next to Back Bay. There are many countries, particularly the dry and the arid, in which storms are a cause for celebration. But nowhere does it quite like Mumbai. I met one of the other writers of this book for dinner in Bandra shortly after, as the rainwater gleamed in treetops and on pavements under streetlights during a break in the downpour. She told me how she and her family had been cooped up in a sweltering house during the summer, with scant relief from electric fans. How the rain was not just a blessing for farmers and those who relied directly on the land, but for people from Mumbai who had endured the monotony of unbearable temperatures, with too little in the way of air-con to lift the weight of the heat. This did not quite explain the beach scenes, however. Perhaps rain was just one among many things that might be used as an excuse to enjoy oneself here. The idea of a population wringing pleasure out of as many things as possible was a theme I would see recurring again and again.

The writer told me how the shape of the city, long and thin, was a curse which meant its 'centre' was placed at its southernmost tip, ensuring that journey times from the suburbs and beyond for commuters were unbearable. The train system cannot cope with the influx of commuters each day, and the unlucky ones are forced to hang onto the sides of the trains. She told me about the times she had the tips of her toes pressed down as the weight of the human cargo bulged into her belly, her fingers hooked around a pole somewhere overhead. She arched her back far beyond the limits of the train doorway, out over the rushing ground. Another writer told me that she had engaged in this activity for fun with an old boyfriend, that they had wanted to experience Mumbai properly. I thought that they had risked their lives for that feeling, and that this must mean that Mumbai was a special

Colaba

Matunga

Churchgate

place. I began to understand why many found the term Mumbai to be cold and meaningless, and preferred Bombay instead, equating the former name with the exterior of the city and the smart face it presents to the modern world, and the latter with intangibles: tastes, colours, pleasures. It begged a question. As an outsider, was I allowed to call the city Bombay? Or would a Londoner bring undertones of colonialism to the word, such undertones the very reason the old Portuguese name was ditched in the first place, with a return to Mum-bai, *Mumbadevi-bai*, patron goddess-mother of this settlement that never stopped growing and evolving. Ought I to stick respectfully to Mumbai? Each time my question was met with genuine amusement. *Just call it Bombay, like we do.*

Mumbai was originally the home of a community of fishermen and their families, the Kolis, spread over an archipelago of seven islands. Leaders and their dynasties succeeded one another, establishing Hinduism and Buddhism here, before King Bhimdev founded his kingdom in the 13th century and lost it to the Muslim rulers of Gujarat decades later. Trade links were established with key centres in the Arab world. The Portuguese interrupted a long period of Islamic influence with the strictures of 100 years of colonial rule. The British wrested the city from their European neighbours under its Portuguese title of Bombaim, or 'good little bay', in 1664. India regained its independence in 1947, and the city was a foothold for the movement.

Communal riots sparked by tensions between the Hindu and Muslim communities, and their complex aftermath, wounded the city in the 90s, after which a brutal attitude toward any hint of urban unrest came into force. These tensions have since largely cleared from the surface of the city's life, and opinions vary as to how deep they may or may not still run. For the most part, these communities and the Christian communities now live together in peace. Smaller religious groups, such as the Zoroastrians and the Iraqi jews, bring their own inimitable stamp to the culture of the city. The former can be traced back to Persia, and their influence can be seen in the striking fire temples which outsiders may not enter, the inimitable Parsi cafés like Zhiyani's and Britannia & Co. Restaurant, and in the ubiquitous Tata brand that has come to symbolise indomitable entrepreneurship. The latter can lay claim to two very beautiful synagogues. The blue edifice of the structure in Kala Ghoda encases a wonderfully still interior, conducive to meditation, yet it sits under watchful military guard.

Around the corner is Kala Ghoda Café, a recent addition to the city that can rival the coffee and the branding acumen of the best cafés from the world's rival megalopoli. The last time I was there, the manager showed me the back rooms that were due to open in the near future, tripling its size and confirming that the customer base for this type of establishment was alive and well in Mumbai. Upstairs, the fashion and homeware boutique Nicobar brimmed with colourful modern interpretations of traditional Indian and Western styles. Bungalow Eight is an innovative shop-cum-exhibition space which features the work of contemporary Indian designers in fashion and furnishings. It is housed in the bowels of Wankhede Stadium, a temple to Indian cricket. Those forging new openings for Indian creativity, via business or the arts, are not doing it in separated, soulless 'districts'. If you want galleries, you need to venture into the bowels of the city itself to find them, and seeking out artworks will teach you about the quotidien details of the place, as it should.

Your journey to a top restaurant will likely not be possible without passing previously unimaginable levels of poverty in side-alleys or beyond the car window. In community after community, the fortunate and the have-nots coexist side-by-side. You could likely create a bubble to protect yourself from empathy here if you wanted to, just as you might in other world cities should you choose to. But in Mumbai you would have to try very hard indeed. The vendors of street food, those who sell trinkets, and those children who solicit donations to their families with a smile and a persuasive pitch, are as restless in their creativity as the new wave of entrepreneurs, who shift pictures around white spaces and serve eggs Parsi-style with espresso.

I wandered into one of the better known art galleries out of sweltering heat on a summer's afternoon in 2016, to find a dimly lit interior and to receive a wiggle of the head from the man on the door when I asked if the space was open for visitors. The ambiguous head gesture, I decided, in this context, meant: 'No, but you can come in if you like'. Inside was high-grade air-conditioning and an installation of pillars which the viewer could walk through, observing as fragments of images painted on them came together when seen from certain angles, causing large-scale pictures to form and break apart again. At one stage, a tap showered tiny LED lights onto a depiction of the city, as though someone had left the waterworks running in the heavens. A young woman appeared at my side and began to explain.

Dhobi Ghat

Mithi River

'We love water here,' she said. 'It is something to be celebrated. It's a link between the old and the new.'

'Mumbai is on the brink of big changes,' I said.

I had the skyline of Marine Drive in my mind, with the sparkling promise of tall new towers hanging far away over the dark ocean. But I found myself talking in clichés.

'Mumbai has always been changing,' she said. 'As long as I've known it.'

She turned out to be the artist of the exhibition, inspecting the set-up the day before its launch. What she might have said to her first visitor was: *you only just got here.*

Overleaf – Back Bay

DADAR

Heart of the City
शहराचा मध्यवर्ती भाग

Photos –
Nirvair Singh Rai

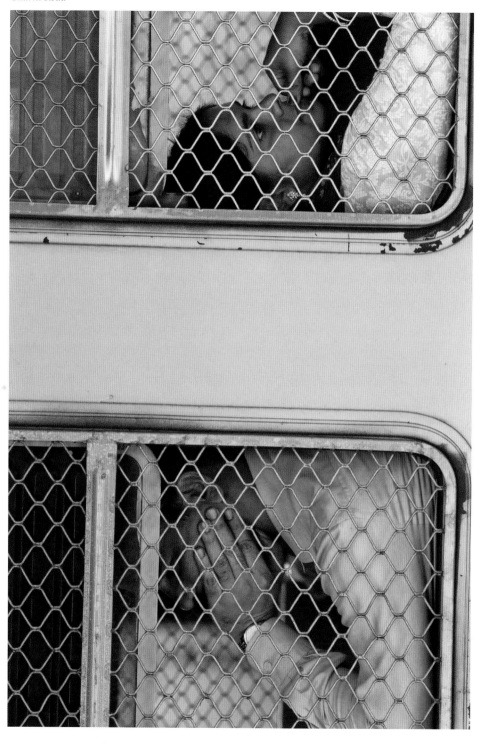

Haji Ali

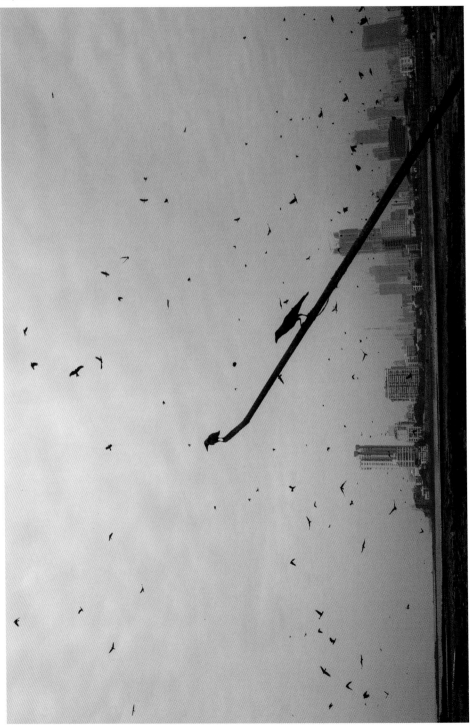

Rajabhi Clock Tower

Marine Drive

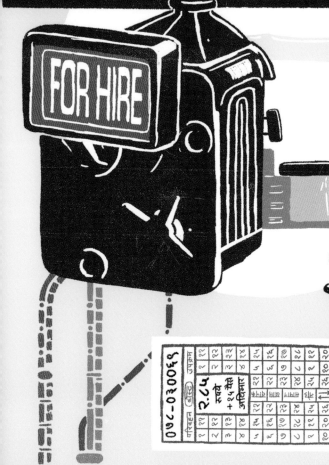

Navigation

जलपर्यटन

Words –
Ambarin Afsar

Photos –
Matthew Smith

Fort

Matunga

There are few places that are physical manifestations of conundrums and contradictions. Mumbai is one of them. The city of dreams, the city of gold, the city where fortune might decide to become one's bedfellow on a whim, or might demand years of toil and hard work. The architecture, culture, food, sights and smells of the city are the culmination of centuries of fantasies, both big and small. Here there are decades-old bakeries run by families alongside the hip artisanal boutiques and craftshops run by young entrepreneurs. Here craft beer rubs shoulders with elder wines and rough, spicy rum, and sports cars get stuck in the same traffic jams as beaten-up scooters. Artists can be found just as easily on the footpaths as in pristine studios, and performers cast their spells on crowded beaches and upscale bars alike.

Mumbai is best experienced at night, when this anthill of teeming millions seems to exhale, offering equal parts silence and noise to the seekers of each. There are pockets to go to when you want to be alone, and others to visit when you long not to be. Stumbling across these can be as simple as taking a quick walk around the area where you're staying. While there is likely to still be some hustle and bustle on the main road, even in the wee hours of the night, the arterial lanes are like treasure troves of the magical and the wonderfully mundane. Here are some pointers for finding your way.

I. BY-LANES OUT OF THE ORDINARY

There are many gems to find here, from leafy community parks, oases a couple of degrees cooler than the rest of the baking city, to tea corners tucked away in the oddest of places. Quaint old houses reminiscent of the Portuguese ancestry of Goa (especially if you're in western Bandra, Khar or eastern Dadar) and vegetable markets with bleary-eyed vendors trying to hawk one last bargain of the day. General and medical stores abound, and it is there that you will also find midnight roadside snacks and tea and biscuits, which only the cast-iron bellies of Mumbai can survive. Here also, you will find the romance of conversation and the company of enthusiastic stray dogs and cats – and their occasional feeders.

2. THE NIGHT'S RITE OF PASSAGE

'Mumbai is safe at night,' some will say. 'Don't go walking alone,' others will say. Trust your instincts and understand the call of the night. Set out prepared with a few maps and take a friend with you. To get a first taste of Mumbai's nights, head to the Queen's Necklace on Marine Drive, keep vigil along with streetlights spitting neon fire, and watch the purple sky turn into hesitant day over the silver and venerable Arabian Sea. Round this off with piping hot, sweet milky tea and well-toasted and buttered bread for breakfast at an Iranian café, and you've been privy to the secret ritual of many heartbroken lovers, sleepless poets and writers, vagabonds and strugglers from all walks of life trying to find their luck in the big city.

3. SCINTILLATING DAYLIGHT

The city offers sanctuary by night, before becoming a vibrant colour palette of all life's hues by day. The sea gleams with hundreds of little suns reflecting off the tops of its modest waves, children run out of school pell-mell with their bright plastic slippers and their uniforms in disarray. Vendors move across the metropolis, making sure that all the cogs in this old machine are well-oiled, their saris and dhotis bright in the midday sun. This is the time when the cool, large halls of libraries and museums seem very appealing. A good lunch, followed by a lazy walk down aisles filled with relics and antiquities from India's rich history, or a ferry ride towards the islands and caves that exist on the fringes of the city, make for a relaxing getaway from the sun.

4. RUSH HOUR

What really defines Mumbai's pace is its rush hour (or hours), which typically range from eight in the morning to midday, and from five in the afternoon to ten at night. While Japan has railway officers who help people into already crowded trains by pushing their bags or coats inside to allow the doors to shut, Mumbai's trains have open compartments and the doors are only used if it is raining very hard or if it is very cold.

The compartments meant for thirty to fifty people each are regularly crammed with double or triple that number. The footboards can accommodate another ten people or so hanging outside the compartment, while window frames offer similar (extremely dangerous) support. Even the space between and above compartments serves as a potentially lethal medium of transport.

Lalbaug Flyover

Nariman Point

But if you're travelling against the flood of commuters at any given time, then taking the train is a good way to beat the on-road traffic, to enjoy some of Mumbai's salty, pungent breezes and to take a gander at the sights and sounds along the way, of which there will be plenty.

Roads are jammed during rush hour. So, before you make a plan for the day, it is best to figure out which direction will you be heading in, whether your journey will occur during rush hour, and whether you can find an alternate route, switch destinations or travel a little earlier or later than you would ordinarily have scheduled. In Mumbai we have the kind of traffic that can make an eight kilometre drive take more than two hours. Catching a train at the wrong time might be life-threatening and, to add insult to injury, you will queue for an age to get on board.

5. THOSE WHO CONDUCT THE CITY

While fleet taxis are pretty reliable, and you're not likely to get fleeced since you have access to the ride estimates beforehand, the true-blue cabbies of Mumbai are the ones who drive its sturdy black and yellow Padminis. Usually, the vehicles are a reflection of the people who drive them. You may find a rosary hanging from the rearview mirror, coupled with a small figurine of Mother Mary or Jesus, or you'll see a *tasbeeh* (an aid to worshipping Allah) oscillating above a small replica of the seaside shrine of Haji Ali, the patron saint of Mumbai, or there will be a garland of fragrant marigolds and jasmine encircling one of the scores of deities who have made India their home.

The kitsch of Mumbai's black and yellow cabs, coupled with their old-world drivers, is second only to the fabulously colourful artwork found on interstate goods vehicles and trucks. Recently, a group of young artists decided to collaborate with Mumbai's cabbies, and create a unique platform to showcase their designs, using taxi seat covers, and the results were nothing short of mesmerising. So, while fleet taxi services might seem more attractive, Mumbai's cabs are where the real charm of the city rests.

The cabbies themselves sometimes know a smattering of languages and are not only very curious about their passengers but might also end up regaling you with tales of their various fares and exploits. All you need to do is initiate the conversation, if you're in a chatty mood.

The overlooked mode of transport in Mumbai is the rickety BEST bus. The colour of the uniforms of most of India's civil service and municipal service personnel is varying shades of mud brown (or *khaki*,

Bandra Kurla

Fort

Matunga

which means 'dust-coloured' in Hindi), and bus conductors and drivers dressed this way make up the second set of men who conduct Mumbai's transport system. Please note that they are notoriously obsessed with receiving exact change when payment for a ticket is made, and can and will ask you to disembark if you do not produce it.

Double-decker buses and open-roof buses are often used to take tourists around the city, but if you wish to avoid the monotony of these pre-decided tours, you can ask the people at your hotel to help you with a bus ride down the sea promenade closest to you. A BEST bus ride is vintage Mumbai, with its bell-chiming indicating the arrival and departure from a stop, the impossible task of standing still as the bus lurches, the salty sea breeze in your hair, and, if you're lucky, old-school paper tickets which look like slips for a lucky draw, or Housie or Sudoku puzzles, with their neatly chequered lists of stops that are punched on the basis of where you intend to disembark.

The third set of equally entertaining people are the auto-rickshaw drivers. These are three-wheeled automobiles that can be quite robust and fast when they want to be, and can also break down, struggle uphill and generally potter around just when you need them to be quick. Some are outfitted with speakers and sub-woofers that would put a DJ to shame, while the lights and décor inside others could embarrass a 70s discotheque. The equal for kitsch and quirks of the black and yellow cabs, these rickshaws run by the meter, though often the meters run twice as fast and need to be cross-verified and double-checked. Insist on going by the meter, regardless of the mode.

6. LEARNING MUMBAI'S COLLOQUIALISMS

Despite the fact that English is spoken widely in Mumbai – it is one official language of India – a good Hindi-to-English dictionary will help you to grasp a few basic terms and phrases, which can prove very handy when trying to break the ice. Watch a few Hindi movies, if you're into that sort of thing, to grasp the dialect. Knowing a little Hindi goes a long way in helping people warm to you, and also warns them against taking you for a ride. Plus, nothing appeals to us sentimental and emotional folk in Bombay more than someone making an effort to be an insider, by speaking our language.

7. THE FAMED INDIAN HEAD WIGGLE

Now, you may or may not have heard about this phenomenon called the 'Indian head wiggle' (also known as the 'yes-no-maybe head shake'), which can confound you at any given point in time. This ubiquitous movement, which involves nodding one's head up and down and sideways at the same time, can mean plenty of different things in different situations. It can imply agreement or intense agreement, disagreement or intense disagreement, apologetic protest, apologetic ignorance and so on.

The key, as someone once put it very well, is not in the hypnotic movement of the head, but in the position of the eyebrows. Upraised eyebrows means interest, curiosity and general positivity, while a gentle frown indicates negativity and disagreement, possibly also confusion. The head wiggle can also be used to call people hither, to ask people to go away, to ask what's up and to acknowledge someone in the first place. You will encounter numerous variations of these and should perhaps even maintain a humorous code or catalogue to help you to decode them. Don't forget to watch the brow and, better still, attempt the wiggle yourself and watch the grins unfold.

8. IN MAPS WE (MOSTLY) TRUST

While maps that can be used on phones are indispensable here, Mumbai often has shortcuts and tiny alleys that are either not recorded, or tagged incorrectly by apps. Having lived here all my life, I was once confounded by a digital map that showed a lane cutting across a small settlement to the main road, which, as it turned out, was only for cyclists and had metal bollards barring autos and taxis from entering. Instead of taking a shortcut, we ended up taking a long-winded route to our destination. Ask shopkeepers, vegetable vendors and cabbies for directions, instead of random passers-by. Usually, stores that make deliveries across the area are more familiar with its various landmarks and by-lanes. Cabbies and rickshaw drivers are helpful and will go the extra mile in helping you to find your destination.

9. THE MELTING POT

North meets West and South meets East in Mumbai's strange, albeit delicious, street concoctions. If your stomach is brave enough to take them on, that is. There you'll come across the little, round, wafer-thin fried dumplings, filled with water spiced with cumin seeds and mint or tamarind, which are known as *pani puri*, and the savoury crepes called *dosas* which are fried in butter and filled with a piping-hot potato

Dharavi

Fort

mash, or *masala aloo*. Mumbai's streets have a lot to offer to people with adventurous palates.

Then there are the corner-shop café gems that offer an authentic taste of the various parts of India. From coconut-based South Indian cuisine, to heavy, rich and aromatic North Indian food, to the minimalism of East India's delicacies and the sweet-and-spicy extravagances of West India, it's possible to sample most of our nation's delights in just one city. There are many multi-cuisine restaurants, too, which are always adapted in the best possible manner to suit the average Indian palate. Almost every dish at these places, regardless of where it has been borrowed from, is given some sort of twist to make it relatable to us Indians, who are fans of explosions of flavour.

10. GET A READ ON THE PLACE

A lot has been written on Mumbai, and books provide some of the best guides to the city. Authors of Indian origin, such as Salman Rushdie, Rohinton Mistry, and Suketu Mehta, have written such fitting records of the place that most others are found wanting. The Ground Beneath Her Feet, The Moor's Last Sigh, A Fine Balance, Family Matters, Midnight's Children, and Maximum City: Lost and Found, take you and your imagination deep into the origins and quirks of Mumbai. All of these works present a side of Mumbai that is as close to the truth as any story can get. Making these your companions will go a long way in helping you understand why the city and its people are the way they are.

11. THE SOUL OF THE CITY

It is not the Arabian Sea, it is not the local trains, it is not the taxis or the buses or the by-lanes or the grimy corners or the pristine promenades that make up the soul of Mumbai, but rather the people. This is an oft-repeated cliché, but, as clichés go, here it is very accurate. The people of this city are street-smart, practical and tough as nails, but they are also warm, accepting and unpredictable in ways both good and bad. They take something that is not to their advantage and work on it until they have made it do what they want it to do. They are persistent, tenacious and do not take no for an answer in life. As a result, you have a strange, mix of people, who are almost always at boiling point, but who also help you when you think no assistance is forthcoming and go out of their way to make you feel welcome, and at home.

This city has been a mistress to generations of travellers, immigrants and fortune-seekers. People come here with dreams in their eyes, and look for their own version of the Indian dream. A major part of the city's largesse comes from its ability to empathise and understand that everyone is just trying to get by here. Mumbai can be ruthless in its darker pockets, and these exist just as much in brightly-lit corporate corridors as out in the streets. But in the city's vibrant, beating heart lie moments of scintillating warmth. What you find here can often be very different from what you set out to seek, but there's a transformative beauty in all of this: the bedrock of Mumbai's landscape.

Overleaf - Horniman Circle

People
लोक

Photos –
Ambarin Afsar

"Bombay is home. Bombay is where the heart is. It is a place that I have embraced for so long that one doesn't know who is holding whom anymore."

Boman

"Mumbai is about freedom, about the ability to choose who I want to be, when I want to be."

Bilquees

"I manage to find work here. I am able to send some money home and make a life for me and my family. While I prefer my village, I can't stay there for too long when I go back, and I yearn to return to the city."

Ashok

*"Mumbai is the sea. I love coming
to the beach and playing with
my brothers."*

Nissa

*"This city is like a hot glass of tea,
and a crumbly caramel pudding. It
melts in your mouth and fills it with
a burning sweetness."*

Dinoo

"Bombay is a place for conversation, for forging new friendships and enjoying the old ones."

Sheila

"All our friends live here. All our lives are centred around here. We can't imagine living anywhere else in the world. Jaisi bhi hai, apni Mumbai hai. (Whatever it is like, Mumbai is our city.)"

Mohammad and Shakeel

"This is such a crowded city, it's crazy, but still it has a heart, where all the goodness is hidden and, sometimes, you can catch a glimpse of it."

Shalu

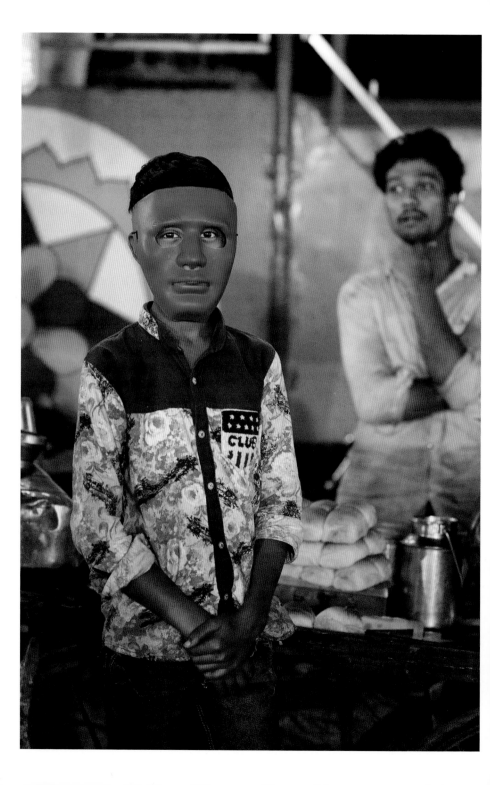

"Mumbai is good for business, if you have the know-how. And also mischief! It is really a city about money."

Afzal

"We wait all year to bring our travelling fair to Mumbai. It is a magical city."

Aakash

Wider City
खोल शहर

Photos –
Nirvair Singh Rai

Juhu Beach

Saint Peter's Church

बडे मिया **Bademiya** Seekh Kebabs ®

Directory
सूची

Words –
Ambarin Afsar
Aditi Dharmadhikari
Avantika Shankar
Matthew Smith

Photos –
Ambarin Afsar
Matthew Smith

CITYSCAPES

शहर भूदृश्य

MATUNGA BACKSTREETS

———

Wandering through Matunga on a bright afternoon can be a curious, dreamlike experience. Many roads and backstreets branch off in all directions, swelling to pleasantly busy one moment, dropping into perfect quiet the next. Fruit and flower sellers offer pastel-coloured wares, matched by the rainbow of spines the booksellers oversee as they watch the day go by. In the hushed ellipses of the backstreets, watch the endless canopies of green play with the sun's rays, sending shadows and spicules of light drifting over the road and the other bystanders who come out to watch you pass: cats, dogs and the ubiquitous crows. Here, a giant bank of ice is cleaned by a man who then drapes a tarpaulin over the top to protect its individual blocks from the heavy sun. There, a cow eyeballs you, wondering what your business is. Nothing more than walking and observing – and perhaps eating. The area is famous for its South Indian cuisine, specifically four restaurants, each of which has its acolytes: Manis, Ram Ashray, Arya Bhavan and the legendary Cafe Madras. They open around 5am, drawing early-risers for their morning coffee and snacks, and provide their own take on dishes such as *dosa*, *pongal* and *upma*. Walking, observing, eating – and worshipping. Matunga was established when Mathangarishi performed the Mahayagnas on the banks of the river Pumpa and was awarded Maharishi status. The Mahayagnas are the five daily sacrifices a Hindu must make to ensure they are in line with their duty to the gods. Many such deities gaze down from Asthika Samaj, a place of worship established in 1923 when a portrait of Lord Sree Ramachandra was hung in the main hall. Such is the number of these otherworldly onlookers that it becomes difficult to tell whether we are distracted by their world, or they are examining ours.

Words – MS | Photo – AA

MAHALAXMI RACE COURSE

There are few places in Mumbai that offer true respite from the daily cacophony of metropolitan life. Usually it is a quiet lane at dawn, at the far end of a sleepy commercial street, or an evening moon shimmering over a small shrine in the backyard of an office complex. Very rarely does it come to those who seek it. However, built on an impressive 225 acres of prime, verdant property, the racecourse is as far a cry from the realities of the city as it is possible to imagine. The road that leads up to it from Mahalaxmi station is often crowded with traffic during office hours, but on entering the racecourse property, you're instantly transported to a lighter, freer world. The Mumbai skyline, just visible from above the canopies of the surrounding trees, appears alien, like another world peering over to see onto your side of the fence. The racecourse, immense as it is in terms of space, appears far more expansive still, to the perspective of one who has just emerged from the crowded intersections of the city. The place is run by the Royal Western India Turf Club, an exclusive group that hosts racing events in both Mumbai and Pune. The course boasts a 2400m race track, a clubhouse for members, an amateur riders' club and permanent stables for the horses, along with a number of restaurants and bars. The very centre of the racecourse – between the oval of the race track – is a public park, which has been meticulously maintained by the RWITC since its inception. In the early mornings, as the race horses are brought onto the track to practice their laps, local joggers come out for their runs, soaking in some sun before the rigorous day ahead. In the evenings, families bring their children, senior citizens have their exercise classes, friends idle around watching the horses, making plans for the night ahead. Stray dogs, veterans of the track, who often run with the horses as they turn into the home stretch, sleep.

Words – AS | Photo – AA

Dr E Moses Marg, Royal Western India Turf Club, Mahalakshmi Nagar 400049

022 2307 1401 | rwitc.com

MARINE DRIVE BY NIGHT

———

Mumbai's residents are sea-worshippers, but not in the religious sense (although during the Ganesh Chaturthi festival Hindus will immerse idols of Lord Ganesha in the water). When the city feels too close, they move towards it. When the rains come in monsoon season, they embrace the sense of release from the strictures of the summer heat by finding more water to be near, and if the Arabian Ocean is crashing against the rocks, sending its spray into the air and adding to the festive feeling, then so much the better. But Marine Drive comes alive every night, regardless of the weather. Gazing across Back Bay from Nariman Point to the farther shore and the glittering skyscrapers that have risen in recent times feels like a way to assess how good the new, improved city has been to you – if, of course, you feel it has improved. Families enjoy the open space of the walkway, parents going over the stresses of the weeks gone by or to come as the children run around oblivious. Young couples who may not have the freedom to express their affection elsewhere in town line the wall that faces the water, whispering, laughing raucously, crying or sitting in silence. In fact, all forms of meditation can fly here, and, despite the busy road that borders the pavement, visitors to Marine Drive by night can move without being on the move. The sparkling lights of the city, old and new, dwindle into the vast darkness of the sea beyond, which fixes the visitor's gaze. The mood is one of wonder. *MS*

THE MANGROVES

———

A large portion of the city of Mumbai has been built on reclaimed land. Up until the 17th century, the area was made up of a group of seven islands, which were later reformed into one continuous landmass. While the topographical changes to the city have been immense, a few clues remain to the city's geographical history. One of the ecosystems that has stuck around from times past is that of the mangroves. The mangroves once extended along the coast and through the various inlets around the city, and were rich with a variety of plant and animals species. Now a good part of the cover has given way to urban development, and most of the larger sections can only be found towards the northern suburbs, along the Vasai and Thane creeks. The Godrej Mangrove Centre in Vikhroli has been established by the Godrej family in an effort to conserve the mangrove cover, and organises tours and nature excursions to encourage education and awareness. Of course, there are still parts of the city's shoreline where the mangroves cane still be found. Carter Road, for example, which is one of the most populated public places in Mumbai, is lined by a small section of mangroves, into which particularly adventurous locals might attempt to wander, and which unfortunately might often be found littered with waste. *AS*

DHARAVI

COLABA CAUSEWAY

A trip around Dharavi is not recommended for the outsider who is without a seasoned guide. The slum concentrates the equivalent population of Birmingham into an area under one square mile. The back-alleys make words like 'labyrinthine' seem quaint, and GPS is unlikely to come to your aid. There is more industry and ambition in this small space than can be found in many whole cities, but very few other than Dharavi's largely sociable teenagers will care to be photographed by a visitor as they go about their daily business. Gawping at poverty will not be appreciated, and it is impossible to visit Dharavi from a developed country without questioning exactly why you are there. Perhaps it is to have your preconceived notion of slumland turned on its head. One further observation about Dharavi: the number of beggars seems to plummet within its confines. *MS*

Colaba Causeway, located in South Mumbai, is a refined version of a flea market. Please do take the descriptor 'refined' with a pinch of salt, since you're just as likely to be assailed by street vendors and hawkers at the Causeway as you are anywhere else in Mumbai. In fact, the one word you'll often find yourself repeating here is, 'no'. However, at the end of your trip, you might still find yourself amazed at the number of trinkets you've gathered, all thanks to the never-take-no-for-an-answer street-entrepreneurs of India. At Colaba Causeway, you will find exotic artefacts rubbing shoulders with affordable and stylish export rejects of popular brands and ornate junk jewellery. The Causeway is home to a market meant both for the traveller who wants a piece of something authentically Indian, but does not want to make too much of an effort for it, and for the Indian who wants to be seen as an equal. *AA*

BANDSTAND

———

Bandstand, one of Mumbai's sea-facing promenades, is a classic example of how it is people, more than any architectural structure, that really make the place. A kilometre long from end to end, it begins just off Hill Road and tapers into the Bandra Fort amphitheatre, followed by the vast expanse of the Arabian Sea. In a city that exhibits a gross disparity in wealth and lifestyle, it is wonderful to have a place where people from all walks of life go to stroll by the sea together. There's an 'Artist's Court' along the promenade, too, which frequently hosts weekend jam sessions and evening sing-a-longs led by street musicians. A walker must weave through *chaiwallahs* on cycles, who offer seemingly-endless quantities of tea and cigarettes, and hawkers selling peanuts and *bhutta* (corn on the cob seasoned with salt and spices), joggers, families and countless couples. Bandstand is referred to as 'Lover's Point' sometimes, owing to the swathe of couples getting cosy by the sea, many of whom don't have anywhere else to go to spend time together, as much of conservative Indian society considers pre-marital relationships taboo.

Bandstand is generous with its space, though, allowing everyone into its dusk-tinged folds as they fade to dark. There's a lovely sense of community, free from the shackles of class, that is so rarely found in Mumbai. Whether you want a small cup of tea to nurse here for an hour, somewhere to catch up with a friend, or just a place to spend some time looking at the meeting of sea and sky, Bandstand will always offer a peaceful spot to those who seek it. *AD*

BJ Road, Bandra West 400050

ARCHITECTURE

वास्तुशास्त्र

HAJI ALI DARGAH MOSQUE

———

Haji Ali's *dargah*, or 'threshold', is the subject of much of Mumbai's lore, myth and legend. There's nothing quite like a romantic story to hold one's imagination, and many such stories are related to the origins of the dargah. The most widely believed of these says that the saint, Sayyed Peer Haji Ali Shah Bukhari, asked for his coffin be set afloat on the sea and buried wherever it came to rest. The dargah was built at the site where it washed up, on a small mound of rocks 500 metres from the shore of Worli, apparently in the middle of the sea. Indo-Islamic architecture benefitted from the Mughal rule and the influx of Persian and Arabian traders. The dargah is one of the finest specimens, and is made predominantly of white marble. It is a source of pride for most citizens not only because it speaks of the seemingly impossible things Mumbai has achieved, but also because it evokes the memory of the Taj Mahal, one of the wonders of the world, which is located in the north of India. The dargah is connected to the mainland by a narrow causeway, nearly a kilometre long, unbound by protective barriers. This causeway gets submerged during high tide, making the dargah inaccessible to devotees. The six-hundred-year-old dargah suffers a great deal of erosion due to the salinity of Mumbai's sea winds that eat at everything, coupled with the collective weight of 80,000 visitors a week. Its main hall is richly carved with patterns and verses of the Qur'an, while its ceiling is embedded with intricate pieces of glass that bear the 99 names of Allah. In the adjacent foyer, or *qawwal khana*, the *qawwals* or sufi singers perform every Thursday or Friday, and are a revitalising sight for stressed and weary eyes. The passionate chanting uplifts one's mood, gives one hope, and bolsters one with all the strength of the sea. In a city that prides itself on instant-everything, this short pilgrimage is one worth undertaking, providing a quick pick-me-up for the soul.

Words and photo – AA

Dargah Road, Haji Ali 400026

022 2352 9082 | hajialidargah.in

RANWAR VILLAGE

——

The aptly named Hill Road, which is one of Bandra's three major roadways, is a perpetual flurry of commercial activity. New businesses spring up every week, and the idle hills of the area, earmarked initially for residential properties, now see their humble tree-lined lancs and narrow streets barely capable of holding the traffic. With the new Rajiv Gandhi Sea Link offering easy access to commuters from South Bombay, the 'crowd' – a term Mumbaikars use not just quantitatively, but also as an indication of character – has magnified. As with most spaces in Mumbai, Bandra grows, evolves, explodes. However, the tenacity of Mumbai's communal establishments continues to hold strong. Even at the edge of a main road brimming over with honking rickshaws and outsized SUVs, there are fruit-sellers who will claim their space. On pavements that see hundreds of pedestrians pass by the hour, there are old bungalows whose doors are left open to the street outside. Signs state matter-of-factly that trespassers will be prosecuted, but otherwise the residents make no attempt to shut out the rest of the world, the way so many city-dwellers elsewhere might do. But there is a unique communal establishment in Bandra called Ranwar Village. With the world now at its doorstep, it is Mumbai's most iconic living anachronism. The village is a vestige of the days when Bandra was made up of independent *pakhadis*, or village settlements, surrounded by rice, coconut and vegetable fields. Ranwar Village once looked right onto the Arabian Sea, but now the land reclamation project has brought it a considerable way inland. Still, the palm trees and salty air, the open leafy courtyards with their pristine white altars to Jesus Christ, and shuttered bungalows with wooden banisters, betray Ranwar's tropical heritage. Occasionally a motorcycle or scooter will pass through a winding lane, but between those minor interruptions, the place is quiet. Neighbours go about their business, cats stare at strangers. A few metres' walk away is the main road, the commercial district. The honking isn't too far off, the demands of city life don't melt away. The city will rage on, as always, but Ranwar stands firm – a memory of a time when the city wasn't so.

Words – AS | Photo – AA | Bandra West

DADABHAI NAOROJI ROAD

Given its colonial roots, many parts of South Bombay have a distinctly European aesthetic. The multitudinous architectural forms that can be found standing side-by-side on the same street is a testament to the city's tumultuous history. A walk down South Bombay's Dadabhai Naoroji Road, also known as the 'Mile Long' road, takes you through parts of the city that appear almost anachronistic, with their massive gothic revivalist and neo-classical buildings pitted against the crowd and energy of a modern Indian metropolis. DN Road starts at Crawford Market, which is a building in the Flemish and Norman styles. The frieze at the entrance, which depicts Indian farmers, and the stone fountains inside, were designed by Lockwood Kipling, who was the father of the novelist, Rudyard Kipling. A walk further down DN Road will take you to the Chhatrapati Shivaji Terminus, formerly known as the Victoria Terminus (the area is still colloquially referred to as 'VT'). The terminus is a massive Gothic building in the centre of an incredible busy cross-section. Surrounded on all sides by structures of equal style and detail, CST still manages to stand apart because of its sheer size – you could imagine it was designed almost pre-emptively for the huge crowds it sees on a daily basis, being the last stop on both the Central and Harbour local train lines. Right across the road is the Times of India building, which holds the press offices of the biggest journal in the country. Just ahead of the Times of India building, flanking the other side of the cross-section, is the headquarters of the Brihanmumbai Municipal Corporation, a building that is most notable for its impressive dome-topped tower. DN Road ends at Flora Fountain, a beautifully sculpted depiction of the Roman goddess Flora, set in the centre of Hutatma Chowk. Although not functional anymore, it is still an impressive sight to behold. *AS*

Dadabhai Naoroji Road, Kala Ghoda, Fort 400001

MANECKJI SETH PARSI AGIARY

BANDRA FORT

This agiary is the second-oldest surviving fire temple in Mumbai, and its facade is a thing of wonder for passers-by. The two winged guardians at the entrance speak of an ancient culture, and a forbidding opulence. The enigmatic aura is enhanced by the fact that only Parsis are allowed to enter fire temples, leaving their interiors shrouded in mystery for outsiders. In 1730, Maneckji Nawroji, the son of an international Parsi trader, arrived in Mumbai from Surat and purchased a large tract of land, upon which he built this structure and also a Parsi colony. In 1803, the temple was badly damaged in a fire, and was rebuilt with the help of donations from wealthy Parsi merchants. It is said that the less well-off devotees offered eggs and mugs of toddy, which were mixed with the reconstruction mortar. Fire temples are built to serve the fires that burn within them, and they are classified and named according to the grade of the fire that they house. *AA*

Perin Nariman Street, Borabazar Precinct, Ballard Estate, Fort 400001

Built by the Portuguese as a watchtower in the early 17th century, to overlook the Arabian Sea to the west and Mahim Bay to the south, parts of the fort endure today as a Grade 1 heritage structure. Bandra Fort has a long and interesting history behind it, but it is the respite it offers from the brutal traffic and general chaos of Bandra that makes it so attractive today. A small gate beyond the Taj hotel leads you inside, with one path leading to the remains of the fort itself, while moulded steps to the left lead into the amphitheatre, a picturesque sea-facing venue that plays host to concerts, classical dance performances, and events such as the Mumbai Festival and Celebrate Bandra. Initially called 'Castella de Aguada' back in 1640, which translates as 'Fort of the Waterpoint', it derived its name from the freshwater spring nearby, where passing ships stopped to source potable water. *AD*

Castella de Aguada, Mount Mary, Bandra West 400050

MAGEN DAVID SYNAGOGUE

———

One of the largest synagogues in Asia, the Magen David Synagogue has been around since 1864, and can be found in the by-lanes of Byculla in South Mumbai. With a name that reads 'Shield of David' in Hebrew, the synagogue was constructed by David Sassoon, the treasurer of Baghdad (and also a man known for his philanthropy and his business acumen in Victorian Mumbai), for Baghdadi Jews who were seeking asylum in India from the oppression of the governor at the time, Daud Pasha. Sassoon worked with local architects, who provided European, revival-era architecture, then-popular in British India, rather than being inspired by local or Middle Eastern styles. Fronted by a high wall and a gate, along a busy road and a congested sidewalk, the cornflower-blue synagogue offers an open, wooded space. Neo-classical features blend with freely-conceived elements, and four columns support the flat-roofed porch. Long, wooden and mesh benches fill the large hall, while the blue and white paint is the result of a recent beautification effort. Home to a small, active congregation, the synagogue sees regular Shabbat morning and holiday services, and is open to the public for a few hours every week. The recently restored synagogue is living proof of the various communities that have contributed to the landscape of Mumbai and to its heritage. *AA*

340 Sir JJ Road, Byculla 400008

022 2300 6675

jacobsassoon.com

THE BOMBAY ART SOCIETY

The Bombay Art Society is the oldest art institution in the Asian subcontinent. First established in 1888, the society has provided a platform for budding Indian visual artists to showcase their work, and, moreover, has created a space in which the public can engage with the various fields of contemporary visual arts. Over the years, the society has partnered with numerous eminent personalities and organisations, and hosted some of the city's most acclaimed cultural events. At the centenary year celebration in 1988, artist MF Hussain performed a live painting, accompanied by the vocals of Pandit Bhimsen Joshi. The painting was bought by the Goodrick Group, the proceeds of which have gone on to facilitate a number of artists' scholarships. Since its inception, the society has hosted one of the city's most widely anticipated visual art fairs, the Annual Art Exhibition, to showcase the work of established, as well as upcoming, artists. While the society used to work out of an office in South Mumbai's Jehangir Art Gallery, which is where the Annual Art Exhibition is held, as a testament to their contributions to Indian culture and heritage, the state government granted them a plot of land in Bandra's Reclamation area, where they now have a three-storey art complex with three galleries, as well as an auditorium, a conference room and a library. Sanjay Puri Architects created the distinctive new home of the institution, in which horizontal and vertical space is merged in one organic form, and light accesses the building through windows that look like the computer panels of the future. *AS*

K. C. Marg, Bandra Reclamation, Bandra West 400050

022 2651 3466

bombayartsociety.org

CULTURE

संस्कृती

VOLTE

———

At the time of writing, Volte was misplaced on Google Maps. Wandering around the neighbourhood of the Bombay Development Directorate chawls (BDD Chawls Worli) is an interesting experience, and, happily, near to the rogue pin on Maps is Amba Devi temple, located in a small cul-de-sac in the streets south of Pandurang Budhkar Marg (PB Marg). Head north and you will find that the building that houses the gallery is not on PB Marg either, despite its official address. When you do get there (ask for directions from the guards at Mahindra Towers), it may not be officially open either. But if someone decides to let you in, you will find that it was worth the journey. In this small, one-room space, we came across some of the strangest and most original pictures we could find in Mumbai. Dreamscapes featuring UFOs, forlorn children and stray members of the animal kingdom. Hallucinatory images of people – and taps – hovering and drifting over dark, icy and volcanic landscapes. A subtle and engaging abstract piece shimmered among them. This 'between-shows' exhibition easily repaid the effort required to find the gallery in a nondescript office building miles from Mumbai's art centre, although we were assured three times that no information on the works or the artists was available, so we cannot share it now. Here's to Mumbai's most intriguing and elusive art gallery.

Words – MS | Photo – AA

202 Sumer Kendra, Pandurang Buhadkar Marg, Worli 40001

022 4096 3300

volte.in

BANGANGA AND VALKESHWAR TEMPLE

———

Legend has it that when Lord Rama was on his way from Ayodhya to Lanka, in pursuit of King Ravana, he was advised to offer prayers to a *Shiva linga*, an abstract representation of Shiva, the Hindu deity. Not being able to find one close by, he made one out of sand. Another legend – or perhaps an extension of the same one – tells of how Lord Rama, who was thirsty but saw around him only sea water, shot an arrow into the ground and let out a tributary of the river Ganga. The religious significance of the Banganga water tank (*baan* means 'arrow', and *banganga* literally means 'Ganga released from an arrow') has not decreased over the many years since its creation. Believed to have been constructed in the 12th century by the Brahmin minister of the Silhara Dynasty, which ruled the area up until the 13th century, the water tank appears a world away from the posh high-rises of Malabar Hill that now surround it. It isn't easy to find an entrance. Through a seemingly random lane, down an inconspicuous set of stairs, you emerge into what could easily be a tableau from another era. The tank itself is a large, rectangular pool flanked on all sides by a set of wide stairs. Local children swim here, priests and worshippers alike bathe themselves before offering their prayers. The waters of the Banganga, like the water of the Ganga itself, are meant to purify one's sins. Small lanes meander around the sides of the complex, lined by living spaces and small shrines. The Valkeshwar Temple complex is on hand. *Valu* means 'sand', and *ishwar* means 'god' – *Valkeshwar* therefore refers to the Shiva linga crafted by Rama, i.e. a god made of sand. The temple itself was constructed around the fabled aid for worship along with the tank, but it was destroyed by the Portuguese before being rebuilt in the 18th century. Over time, a number of other temples have come up around the area, some smaller and less conspicuous than others, each one helping to support the immense religious and cultural history that holds the place together.

Words – AS | Photo – AA

Banganga Cross Lane, Teen Batti, Malabar Hill 400006

THE LIBERTY CINEMA

———

Built in 1947, The Liberty Cinema is one of Bombay's last art deco single-screen theatres. Mr. Habib Hoosein, its founder, derived its name from the nation's then-imminent independence. Located in the heart of South Bombay, it has a long, illustrious history behind it, leading up to its status as a cultural centre today. The grandeur of the place – it is acknowledged as a Grade 2A heritage building – is one thing that the ravages of time haven't been able to strip away, despite its difficult journey through history. The coved ceilings, carpeted interiors, and the magnificent Plaster of Paris ornamentations are bound to make your jaw drop as you step into the velvet-lined lobby. A small kiosk sells popcorn here, and the space is filled with stalls of books and merchandise when the theatre hosts film festivals, such as the annual Kashish Mumbai International Queer Film Festival, South Asia's biggest such event. Initially opened to screen Hindi films in an age when most of the theatres in South Bombay would only screen English language films, the Liberty has since thrown open its doors to myriad cultural activities, including stand-up comedy and music concerts, whilst retaining a special focus on world cinema. Inside, the 1,200-seater auditorium faces a majestic stage flanked by two frozen, golden fountains. As the ivory-coloured curtain falls at the end of the each show, the Liberty reminds you of the ways in which an authentic cinematic experience can move you. *AD*

41-42 Marine Lines 400020

022 2208 4521

thelibertycinema.com

NATIONAL GALLERY OF MODERN ART

———

Here you will find temporary exhibitions which delve deep into the work of modern Indian artists. The open-plan spaces are linked by staircases, breaking up the substantial shows in a helpful manner. But if you only have time for a short visit, head to the dome-ceilinged upper floor to find a superbly curated sample of the gallery's permanent collection. A brief but powerful summary of the way in which the familiar tropes of modern art intersected with the Indian visual tradition reveals the eminence of landscape in the cultural imagination. In one painting, industrial workers gaze towards the ground whilst mountains cradle the light majestically in the distance, apparently out of reach. Entitled 'Road Building Work at Kalka', and painted by Bhupen Khakkar, we are left to wonder whether the road newly laid will lead towards these natural marvels, or whether it will bypass them. Other works reduce the strata of landscapes to near-abstract worlds, inner terroir for the mind to drift through. Hinting at cultural paths taken and paths to come, the paintings face each other in the circular space, sparring with one another, with the Western tradition, and with the visitor's imagination. MS

Sir Cowasji Jahangir Public Hall, MG Road, Fort 400032

022 2288 1969

ngmaindia.gov.in

JAMA MASJID

———

Located in the heart of one of Mumbai's busiest commercial districts, the Crawford Market, is the city's largest mosque, the Jama Masjid. Demolished at its original location and relocated here in 1775, the mosque was erected with the permission of the landowner, a Muslim merchant from the Konkan region, who traded in Goa and Calicut. He agreed to the construction, on the condition that the large water tank situated in the midst of the land was to be preserved intact. It was this condition that gave birth to a unique one-storey mosque, built on the emerald green waters of a 10-foot deep tank, fed by springs, and home to fish and turtles. The eastern gate leads across an open courtyard to the ancient tank, which now has steps and embankments, and from the depths of which rise sixteen black stone arches, constructed in 1874, that support the mosque. The incongruence of the green pool overlooked by an ornate, carpeted, marble prayer hall, and the otherworldliness of this combination, leave you feeling a little disoriented. The year of the mosque's completion can be found in a chronogram that reads

jahaz-i-akhirat, which translates as 'the ship of the afterlife', or 'the ship of the world to come', alluding to the mosque and the tank on which it is built. Visit Jama Masjid, and you will have the distinct impression that you've walked into the halls of the underworld, from which all life springs forth. *AA*

Sheikh Memon Street, Chippi Chawl, Kalbadevi 400002

022 2342 5453

DEEPAK CINEMA

———

Deepak Cinema is easily one of the most heartening revival stories that Bombay has witnessed in the recent past. The 90-year-old theatre was transformed just a few years ago from an erstwhile landmark built on ancestral property in Worli, to a haven for arthouse cinema. After buying tickets outside, the iconic archway ushers you into a spacious courtyard where two white stone statues of elephants stand guard. A small café in the corner caters to visitors with a range of finger-food, and the sprawling seating area offers one a chance to sit and enjoy the late afternoon sunlight playing on the patterned roof before heading in for the film. The 500-seater theatre has screened everything from Rashomon to Breakfast at Tiffany's, and their next announcement is always awaited with much anticipation by the small but steady stream of regulars. The cinema house got a new lease of life when its third-generation owner, well aware of its vintage charm, had the theatre refurbished in 2014, being careful to retain its inimitable aesthetic. He also set up Matterden (from 'matter' and 'den', denoting dark energy), in collaboration with the Enlighten Film Society, a creative company made to produce and to distribute independent and arthouse films for the average cinema-goer, amongst other services. Close to a century after declaring their small ticket window open, Deepak Talkies' biggest achievement yet has been to safeguard its vision for its own future. *AD*

NM The Deepak, 38, N M Joshi Marg, BDD Chawl, Lower Parel 400013

022 2492 3399

deepakcinema.com

PROJECT 88

———

When Project 88 was founded in 2006, the Indian art scene was undergoing a transformation. There was a need to break away from the past and establish a foothold in the contemporary art world. So Project 88 focused all its energies on the emerging generation of artists, developing, over this last decade, an eclectic list of creatives. The building housed a printing press in its previous life and now the space boasts a minimal, cavernous interior with curved metal beams and iron pillars. From mixed media works, drawings and video, to sculpture, graphic novel art and installations, via book readings, Project 88 offers a fluid space that is unafraid to present a modern vision of Indian creativity. *AA*

BMP Building, Narayan A Sawant Road, Azad Nagar, Colaba 400005

022 2281 0066

project88.in

NATURE

नसिर्ग

SANJAY GANDHI NATIONAL PARK

———

Located within the northern borders of Mumbai, and surrounded on three sides by some of the most densely populated suburbs of the city, Sanjay Gandhi National Park has often been referred to as the 'lungs' of the metropolis. Over the years, Mumbai has expanded to the point where the distinction between city and suburb has blurred, and the national park which was once a way to escape the city is now enveloped by the urban machine. Still, it is a massive expanse of forest, a much-needed green filter for the city's pollution and a break from the urban heat. It makes up a good twenty percent of the area of Mumbai. This expansive 104 square kilometre national park is one of the most visited parks in Asia, not least because of its location. It is a favourite among nature clubs, wildlife enthusiasts and schools conducting field trips. The park offers a number of activities for tourists, some of which should be booked in advance to ensure availability. The Nature Information Centre has been set up with the express purpose of educating visitors about the various plant, bird and animal species that are found in the park, and the massive ecosystems that are contained by it. The centre offers nature trails, butterfly and birdwatching excursions, and even overnight camping trips, with the aim of promoting environmental awareness among visitors. There are lion and tiger safaris that take you around the park in enclosed vehicles. Another of the primary attractions is the Kanheri Caves system. This 2000-year-old site was built to provide a place for understanding Buddhism, and a large part of the complex still stands today. The trek up through the caves is a long one, though not devoid of amusement – the ruins are home to a large band of monkeys, who interact eagerly with tourists, and seem to have perfected the art of stealing their food. The Gandhi Tekdi, a monument to Mahatma Gandhi, is another key destination to trek up to. It offers a beautiful bird's-eye-view of the park, as well as the city.

Words – AS | Photo – AA

022 2886 0362

sgnp.maharashtra.gov.in

MADH ISLAND

Beyond the point where the local Mumbai railway line ends in the north at Malad, Madh Island sprawls quaintly and lazily into farmlands and small fishing villages. The quiet charm of Madh island is reminiscent of the countless Konkani villages lining the Western coast of the country, replete with tiny, undulating lanes fringed with waving palm trees. Koli fishermen, East Indian Roman Catholics and the Marathi community have lived together in this little paradise for years, and the island is a favourite amongst the Bollywood film and advertising industry for shoots, be it on the lesser-known Dana-Pani beach, where locals can often be found engrossed in a game of cricket, or in the various massive bungalows that are available to be rented out. While local transport and hire cars are available, if you're feeling adventurous, renting a bicycle to explore the area is much more of a treat. The air here is often pungent with the smell of fish from the nearby ice factories, and time seems to stand still as you watch fishing boats bob merrily in the distance. Hotels like The Retreat and The Resort are popular among travellers over weekends, but visiting Madh Island during the weekdays when it is less crowded is more sensible. Besides simply soaking up the sun and fresh air away from the manic pace of the city, there is the restored 500-year-old Church of St. Bonaventure, built in the 15th century, that's definitely worth a visit, as well as a centuries-old Portuguese fort. Perhaps it is because Madh Island rests so closely to nature, and contains so much empty space, a rarity in the shoulder-to-shoulder city it adjoins, that, as dusk fades to night, there are several ghost stories that do the rounds amongst the locals. And if the road seems a little too long on the way back, you always have the option of taking a boat from the jetty, which will take you direct to the bustling heart of Versova.

Words – AD | Photo – AA

A1, Madh, Marve Rd, Christian Wada, Madh 400061

GIRGAUM CHOWPATTY BEACH

In a city starved of open spaces, the Arabian Sea brings a blast of fresh air, literally and figuratively. As well as the refreshing, albeit fishy, breeze, it also provides promenades and beaches that act as communal spaces for residents, as well as tourist attractions for those living in land-locked areas of the country. Girgaum Chowpatty is located in South Mumbai, at the beginning of Marine Drive, or the 'Queen's Necklace', and it is one of the more popular beaches of the city. It plays host to plenty of street food stalls, vendors hawking all sorts of toys, masseuses who offer head massages and a menagerie of Indian tourists. Occasionally, seagulls are visible, bobbing on the diamond-topped waves of the afternoon sea. The word *Chowpatty* originates from 'chau-pati' or four channels or creeks, and the place really does seem like a confluence of sorts. Many a troubled soul has found solace in the noise of the sea and the city that seem to merge here into a unique cacophony that sounds like company. Lined up across the road are elegant, art deco buildings with curving balconies, ornate motifs and symmetrical facades. In fact, Mumbai has the second largest art deco district in the world, superseded only by Miami. A freewheeling milieu that consists of visitors, college students, joggers and hawkers, moving among these effortlessly stylish grand residences, makes Girgaum Chowpatty an eclectic beach pick. The sea is accessible at all times of the day, though nocturnal visitors may be shooed away by cops working the night shift. *AA*

FIVE GARDENS

Smack in the heart of the city, Dadar is easily one of the most densely-populated areas of Mumbai. The Dadar Parsi Colony, the largest Zoroastrian enclave in the world, is home to a cluster of five large gardens, separated by winding roads lined with trees. Step into these lush, green spaces and the drop in temperature is palpable as you exit Mumbai's muggy heat. Probably one of Bombay's better-kept secrets, Five Gardens, under its fluttering green canopy, reminds you to breathe in a way few other places in the city can. Each garden has been taken over by a different crowd of regulars: groups of children frolic in the playground areas situated in one, while musclemen execute push-ups with steely determination in another. If you're lucky, you're likely to come upon a group of young people slack-lining in a third, the ropes they navigate strung taut from one mammoth tree to another, as other visitors watch them from the benches nearby, emanating puffs of smoke. Those who grew up in the area fondly recount blissful evenings with old Parsi 'uncles' blasting rock music from their cars as they enjoyed an evening drink after a long day of work. There are even whispers of Freddie Mercury of Queen, born Farrokh Bulsara, visiting the gardens occasionally for a spliff when he was staying with a relative in the area. No visit to Five Gardens is complete without a stop at the hawkers stationed around the gardens, offering Bombay's famous *chaat* dishes as well as ice *golas* (lollies). The *kala khatta* ice gola is an enduring summer favourite, a cold blackcurrant confection that is as sweet as it is earthy. *AD*

Mancherji E Joshi Chowk, Central Railway Colony, Dadar East 400014

THE MAIDANS

———

The old esplanade of Bombay was once an open stretch of land that overlooked the Arabian Sea. In the mid-19th century, it provided ground for defences that flanked the fort once situated here, shielding its structure against potential attack from the west. Once the fort was torn down, the area became the city's promenade and a recreation ground. Today, the maidans – broken by stretches of Mahatma Gandhi Road and VN Road – offer South Bombay some respite from the ever-increasing traffic and crowds. Azad Maidan, which makes up a part of the playing ground around the Bombay Gymkhana, is a popular site for sports, and a field for the city's inter-school competitions. Oval Maidan, overlooked by the enchanting Gothic Revival edifice of the Mumbai High Court at one end, and a stretch of art deco residentials at the other, has been restored by the residents' association and is now a popular spot for evening walks and picnicking families. Cross and Cooperidge Maidans serve as cricket and football fields for local students. Mahatma Gandhi Road, which flanks Cross Maidan

to the west, has been nicknamed 'Fashion Street' because of the string of roadside clothes stalls that see hundreds of visitors every day. For peace and quiet, keep on the grass. *AS*

Mahatma Gandhi Road, New Marine Lines, Marine Lines 400020

GORAI BEACH

There aren't a lot of beaches around the city of Mumbai that aren't overrun by crowds, or murky with the pollutants of the metropolis. For a lot of the city's inhabitants, the coast is never more than a few minutes' drive away, but access to a clean, visitor-friendly beach is surprisingly rare. Most Mumbaikars tend to get away from the city when they feel the need to soak in some sun. Gorai Beach, named after the village of Gorai, makes for a popular weekend getaway. It isn't too long a drive from the international airport, and once you cross the main suburbs of the city, the road is quite pleasant and green. Alternatively, it can be accessed by ferry from Versova. There is still untouched land here, although a large part of the area has now been developed to make way for private resorts, hotels and holiday homes. Besides the beach, there are a number of other attractions around the area that might encourage a longer stay, like the Tansa Wildlife Sanctuary and Arnala Fort. A cycle tour is recommended – or why not cycle to Gorai from Mumbai? Then at least you'll have earned your time beside the waves, as well as seeing how the Big Smoke and nature segue into one another here. *AS*

HORNIMAN CIRCLE

———

Occasionally a feature of the
urban landscape will serve as
a cross-section of the history of
the area in which it is situated.
Horniman Circle is named for
Benjamin Horniman, once editor
of the Bombay Chronicle and a
freedom fighter who supported
India's independence from the
British Empire. In the 1840s, a
couple of decades after it was
first constructed, it was used as
an area to offload coconut shells
amongst other refuse. One of the
governors who sought to beautify
it was Lord Elphinstone, hence
it took on the name Elphinstone
Circle in the 1870s. Historically,
the Parsi community have used
this small park as a spot for social
gatherings, and Sufi mystics still
hold the Ruhaniyat festival here
annually. Come to sit and read
the papers with businessmen on
their lunch break, or simply to
find some shade in this perfect
pocket of green, which keeps to
itself in the heart of busy Kala
Ghoda. *MS*

HOTELS

हॉटेल्स

ABODE BOMBAY

———

This hotel sits in the jumbled backstreets that lead out from Colaba, past the legendary Regency Cinema, to the Gateway of India and the open sea. Stationed near local favourites such as Café Mondegar, Indigo and The Table, it is perfectly suited to travellers looking for well-appointed accommodation with high levels of comfort and service, but without the big-budget five-star hotel approach. It calls itself Mumbai's first boutique hotel, and, whether or not this is true, it is perhaps the first hotel in the city to successfully blend the heritage of Indian design with contemporary expectations, and finish up with an endearing and stylish residence for visitors to the city. Almost every item that adorns the place has been sourced from Indian designers and companies. Attention to detail is relentless: beautiful copper water jugs and wicker furniture seem to reference styles both past and modish effortlessly. The chairs, tables and ottomans have been sourced from second-hand markets and then restored, or commissioned especially from skilled artisans. Shelves in the lobby and elsewhere reference the packed bookcases that can be seen at roadside vendors across the city, and the floors of the rooms are wonderfully cool underfoot, the result of cement tiling laid using a 100-year-old technique. The reception area doubles as the dining room, where guests drink coffee and eat, choose books from the library at hand or chat to the staff of the hotel, who offer a wealth of knowledge about Mumbai. Room rates vary from reasonable to the more expensive for a few extra features such as a standalone bath, lounge area and desk, so there is something to suit every budget. In its own unique way, Abode has made a new gateway to India – or to this particular city, at least – that a certain type of traveller was missing.

Words and photo – MS

RRR

Lansdowne House, M.B.Marg, Apollo Bunder, Colaba 400039

080 8023 4066 | abodeboutiquehotels.com

THE OBEROI

———

Although its main competitor sits regally at the Gateway of India, soaking up much of the attention when it comes to luxury hotels in Mumbai, The Oberoi can lay claim to the more exceptional positioning, lying at the southern end of the 'The Queen's Necklace', or Marine Drive. Here Mubaikars, rather than tourists, come to take in the night-time air, and by day the view of the ocean is unimpeded. The Oberoi features bright, spacious rooms that are as fresh and modern as they are homely and comfortable. Ziya, the hotel's prized restaurant, is one of the best in the city, offering genuinely inventive Indian cuisine. The central positioning of the hotel also allows travellers to retreat periodically from the hectic atmosphere of central Mumbai to a place where calm and serenity reign. This tranquillity may be a little much for some – other hotels in the city have busier bars, more families crowded around the tables, a livelier pool scene. But the Trident is next door, if that's what you're after. The Oberoi's impeccable service is only enjoyed by the high-end business crowd at present, as evidenced by the electronic gates and the requirement for vehicles to open their trunks upon entry. The pool outside is small but perfectly formed, allowing for afternoon swims that provide space for you to reflect on your day, often with only the crows for company. In one of the busiest cities you're ever likely to visit, The Oberoi provides more than the obvious luxuries.

Words – MS | Photo – AA

RRRRR

216 Netaji Subhash Chandra Bose Rd, Churchgate 400021

022 6632 5757

oberoihotels.com

LE SUTRA

―――

Filled with contemporary Indian art, collected by a team of artists, designers and curators, Le Sutra sits atop Carter Road in the suburb of West Bandra. It claims to be the first Indian art hotel and has fourteen rooms based on mythological characters and religious figures, such as the Buddha, Emperor Ashoka and Ravana. Each of these characters stands for a certain set of values, and the décor is based on characteristics such as sensuality, purification, and love. Each floor represents a level of spirituality. The higher the floor, the more transcendent the state of mind. The hotel also boasts a spa service, and is attached to two fine-dining restaurants: Out of the Blue, which serves a variety of continental food, and Olive Bar & Kitchen, a perennial Mumbai favourite, famed for its Mediterranean cuisine. Interestingly, the director Baz Luhrmann has painted a mural on the entrance of Le Sutra, a fact that only adds to the artistic experience that Le Sutra offers the traveller who is looking for aesthetic stimulation. *AA*

RRRR

14 Union Park, Khar West 400052

022 2649 2995

lesutra.in

JW MARRIOTT JUHU

Located a short walk away from the Prithvi Theatre in Juhu, one of Mumbai's premiere destinations for drama, the JW Mariott is glitzy in a good way, if that's your cup of tea. Frequented by A-list celebrities and the who's who of Mumbai, it offers not just a spa, but also a private beach, a luxury that is almost unheard-of in the city. The hotel is home to some of the finest rooms in Mumbai, with the Royal Lotus suite offering an unfettered view of the Arabian Sea, the pool below, and a stretch of the sandy shore. Dining options include: breakfast at the Bombay Baking Company, a charming bakery that offers books, teas, homemade bread, artisan sandwiches and pastries; brunch or lunch at Mezzo Mezzo, which brings Tuscany and a taste of Southern Italy to India; high tea at the Executive Lounge; cocktails and tapas at Arola, a club that offers the best of Mumbai's famed nightlife along with an abundance of Spanish culinary treats. *AA*

RRRRR | Juhu Tara Road 400049

022 6693 3000 | marriott.com

TAJ MAHAL PALACE AND TOWER

Aesthetic purists take flight – here is a mish-mash of myriad styles and ideas. Building inspired by the Taj Mahal? Check. Glittery Chinese and Japanese restaurants? Check. Luxury stores built into its halls? Of course. Patrons of every nationality coalesce by the pool, a dreamlike spectacle when glimpsed on champagne-blurred nights through a half-open door. Women in niqabs rub shoulders with tourists from Japan and the West as suitcases stack up behind reception and the assured staff exercise subtle control over the chaos. To be found on the ocean front, this particular incarnation of the Taj brand is opulent indeed, but it seems very much rooted in the bustle of the city streets, as guests flow in and out, chattering and laughing. It is still the only show in town for many accommodation-seekers as, more than most hotels, it appeals to all the family, and it embodies a genuine sense of fun. *MS*

RRRRR | Apollo Bandar, Colaba 400001

022 6665 3366 | taj.tajhotels.com

GRAND RESIDENCY HOTEL AND SERVICED APARTMENTS

In a city like Bombay, where peak traffic time can mean hours stuck in gridlock, Grand Residency Hotel and Serviced Apartments gives you the option of staying north of the centre if this is where your activities will be based. The seven-floored establishment has various types of accommodation: a Deluxe Room; Studio; One-Bedroom; Two-Bedroom Apartments. Most of the rooms have living- and dining-room areas in addition to a smart kitchenette that is fully-equipped and replete with complementary fruit and cookies which are restocked every day. With the airport close by, along with Bandra Kurla Complex, the hotel makes sense for business professionals looking for a Bandra base. Travellers who are here for adventure will have a plethora of places to investigate, from Mount Mary's Church, to the market and shopping areas, not to mention Bandra's hidden coffee and food spots and its famed sea-facing promenades. *AD*

RRR | Junction of 24th and 29th Road, Off Turner Road, Bandra West 400050 022 6710 6000 | grandresidency.com

THE TRIDENT AT BANDRA KURLA

Bandra Kurla Complex has now emerged as one of Mumbai's leading business districts. Having taken the spotlight off of South Bombay's traditional commercial areas, BKC symbolises the city's continual northward expansion. Not only does it house a large number of the city's main corporate offices, but it has become a cultural centre as well, with its fair share of bars, restaurants, cafés and nightclubs. True to Mumbai's identity as a burgeoning global city of commerce, Bandra, and BKC in particular, houses the largest percentage of the city's expat population and its business travellers. The Trident at Bandra Kurla Complex is, as a natural consequence, one of the busiest hotels in the city. Designed specifically to cater to corporate guests, the hotel is mere minutes away from the business district and less than a half-hour from the airport. *AS*

RRRRR

C 56, G Block, Trident Road, Bandra Kurla Complex 400051

022 6672 7777 | tridenthotels.com

SHOPS

———

दुकाने

VARIOUS AT DHOBI TALAO

———

On peering into the sleek, polished-wood-framed store front of Various at Dhobi Talao, you'd imagine you were looking into an artist's studio, or (were it not on the ground floor and open to the winding lanes of one of Mumbai's oldest commercial districts), a young, urban-millennial's living room. The space is bereft of the flamboyant window tableaux and the heavily curated display-tables that one commonly associates with designer shops. There seems to be almost no effort, either, to keep the store space distinct from the bustle of the street outside – the city intrudes through the wide, spare windows. The furniture is beautifully crafted – modern, yet with a touch of those slender, sensual contours so unique to Eastern architecture. The smaller design objects, too – multipurpose wooden blocks and vases, sleek, minimalist brass platters – are what one might call modern, but they are still wholly Indian, paying homage to traditional forms. Various is inviting in a way that stores usually are not, and homes usually are. There isn't much choice, but this is the store's strength – a visitor might take their time to inspect every shape and line, to experiment with the purposes of the pieces on offer. Various, as its name suggests, was conceived of as an environment where a multitude of art, design and craft works could be showcased, used and discussed. By night, the space invites artists and creators to come together, to share their work and their cultural ideas. The studio that designs most of its products is based in Ahmedabad. Various at Dhobi Talao is its first retail store.

Words – AS | Photo – AA

1 Meghji Bhavan, Barrack Rd, Dhobi Talao, New Marine Lines 400020

022 2205 2743

variousatdhobitalao.in

AHMED JOO

———

Tucked into a quiet lane behind the Taj Mahal hotel sits Ahmed Joo, a shop selling antiques and 'curios', painted on the outside with the vibrant blue and pristine white of an aesthetic brought to Bombay by the Portuguese. Inside, there's a little waiting area, with old leather couches and rugs, reminiscent of vintage Mumbai when luxury meant a lot of wood and leather. The second thing you see is a door covered by a curtain. Peek through, and it feels like you are looking into Aladdin's cave of treasures. Warm lighting, lots of glass, crystal, semi-precious and precious artifacts line the shelves and the tables. There's something for most connoisseurs looking to take back an authentic piece of Indian history, or simply something remarkable from somewhere further afield. The choice seems infinite, from beautiful swiss clocks to miniature deities and bewitching pieces of jewellery. If you are lucky, you might be regaled with the tale of how the particular object of your interest found its place in Ahmed Joo's venerable hoard of old gold.

Words – AA | Photo – MS

Ormiston Road, Apollo Bandar, Colaba 400001

0122 762 6189

No website

NICOBAR DESIGN STUDIO

———

The alleys of Kala Ghoda have become a hub of culture and commerce in recent years. A walk through the by-lanes will take you past a slew of newly launched concept cafés and artsy lifestyle stores. A once sleepy neighbourhood is bursting with life. Still, one does come across a few islands of calm amidst the clatter of rapid gentrification. Right across from the renowned Trishna restaurant, and above Kala Ghoda Café, sits Nicobar. Named after the Andaman and Nicobar Islands, the brand draws its design inspiration from the playful simplicity of the tropics, with allusions to a breezy island lifestyle. Nicobar seamlessly blends its Indian roots with a contemporary, relaxed aesthetic, a concept that acts as a refresh for contemporary Indian fashion. Banana palms line its large windows, an easy jazz playlist unwinds and everywhere one finds a soothing, earthy décor. The apparel – which ranges from saris and *kurtas* to shirt-dresses and slouchy pants – is a mélange of rich, organic cottons, linen and *khadi*. One of the most iconic pieces is the polka dot maxi-dress, an example of the brand's ability to weave the quirky and the casual, playfully. Nicobar also has a collection of products for the home, from dinner sets and serveware to cushions, table linen, bedding and home décor. Possibly one of its most innovative lines is its travel collection. Bags, pouches, organiser cases and other packing essentials extend its dreamy, wanderlust aesthetic to new forms and functions. The space speaks to a growing culture of young Indians, familiar with the world beyond their homeland, in effortless conversation with it. *AS*

10 Ropewalk Lane, Above Kala Ghoda Café 400001

022 2263 3877

nicobar.com

KITAB KHANA

———

With a name that translates as the house (*khana*) of books (*kitab*), this boutique bookstore provides a selection of works across all genres, curated by a special advisory panel. Its beautiful wooden interior and mezzanine evoke the distinct feeling of one's having walked into a library. Housed in a 150-year-old heritage structure, the shop conjures an old-world charm that is missing from most commercial book chains. There is a little area set aside for children and, interestingly given its austere facade, the bookstore also features a vegetarian café. It stocks English literature as well as Indian, coffee table books and the reference sections one would expect. Occasionally, there are theatre, art and music workshops and performances, and the ambiance, the smell of freshly brewed coffee and the caramel smell of books all come together to create a welcome haven for dedicated page-turners. *AA*

M45-47 M.G. Road, Somaiya Bhavan, Ground Floor, Fort 400001

022 6170 2276 | kitabkhana.in

CHIMANLALS

———

An almost unidentifiable shop in one of the cosier by-lanes in Fort, Chimanlals has been leading the handmade paper goods industry for over half a century. As you enter, you're surrounded by a wealth of colour lining the walls – stacks upon stacks of notepaper, wrapping paper, gift bags, letterheads and more, all richly coloured and textured. Chimanlals has also extended its repertoire to include desk organisers and collapsible baskets. The beauty of the products on display is that each and every design has a history and relevance that has been meticulously researched and curated, drawing inspiration from a variety of traditional sources – the *ikkat, bandhani, warli* manufacturing styles and more. It has helped to create the new market for *kagzi*, or paper handmade with an ancient Indian technique that they aim to keep alive. The store is nirvana for anyone who loves stationery, and it is ideal for gifting. *AS*

A-2 Taj Building, 210 D.N. Road, Fort 400001

022 2207 7717 | chimanlals.com

BUNGALOW EIGHT

LE MILL

Hidden incongruously beneath Wankhede Stadium, temple to Indian cricket, is a hip independent boutique showcasing the work of a variety of Indian designers. Finely crafted furniture, clothing, blankets, pieces of home décor and jewellery are laid out in a spacious area so delicately presented that guests are required to remove their shoes. Setpiece displays that gather up work from the various contributors are quite remarkable in themselves. But don't mistake this superlative curation for the work of assistants in a design museum. Bungalow Eight's wares are very much for sale, with prices ranging from the positively luxurious to the much-more-affordable. *MS*

Inside Wankhede Stadium, North Stand, E & F Block, D Road, Churchgate 400020

022 2281 9880

bungaloweight.com

Through an anonymous doorway on an otherwise crowded side street near the Gateway of India, and up a winding flight of stairs (the base of which has been stencilled with cryptic hashtags), Le Mill's interior opens up as a surprise for the first-time visitor. It is spacious, with the white-and-black décor perfectly offsetting the vibrant displays and the upbeat electronic music. The store was founded with the intention of curating eclectic designer lifestyle products – from home furnishings and tableware to clothes and jewellery – that are made in India by independent designers who aren't necessarily widely accessible. Le Mill also throws in the occasional international label – Balenciaga and The Row, among others – and retails them at the international selling price, without passing on the import duty to customers. The store holds the occasional cultural event, which makes it a space worth watching. Le Mill is a pioneer in Indian retail. *AS*

Pheroze Building, Chhatrapati Shivaji Maharaj Marg 400005

022 2204 1926 | lemillindia.com

CAFÉS

कॅफे

KALA GHODA CAFÉ

———

Turning the corner past the cornflower blue of Knesset Eliyahoo synagogue off Ropewalk Lane, early in the morning, builds a rising sense of anticipation. Stationed alongside Nicobar on this otherwise charmingly shabby backstreet is the smartly branded and well-appointed, undisputed number-one purveyor of espresso-based coffee in Mumbai. The familiar international tropes of such a place can clearly be observed here. Young entrepreneurs and the occasional Westerner creep in shortly after opening time. Well-dressed mums occupy the seats from mid-morning to lunch. After that, finding a seat can be tricky – or at least, it used to be. A new back area with capacious accommodation for guests has recently been unveiled. The demand shows that Mumbai is fertile ground for anyone wishing to bring fashionable coffee shops to the city. At the time of writing, it has little competition. But caffeine-orientated visionaires beware: Kala Ghoda Café serves a mean double espresso, with food that befits its hometown, including highly serviceable helpings of *Parsi Pora* (a spicy omelette). The cookies aren't bad either.

Words – MS | Photo – AA

10 Ropewalk Lane, Opp Trishna Restaurant, Kala Ghoda, Fort 400001

022 2263 3866

kgcafe.in

B MERWAN & CO.

———

Among the oldest surviving Irani cafés in Bombay, B Merwan & Co. has carved its own niche in the cultural stone of the city. Located opposite South Mumbai's Grant Road railway station in a run-down edifice, the café is always bustling with a range of customers: daily wage earners, raucous schoolchildren, brusque sari-clad women, young working professionals, a few mavericks and the occasional millennial visitor looking for some old-world charm to accompany his chai. The high ceilings, with exposed wooden beams, overlook a large room decked in floral tiles and filled with marble-topped tables and the vintage bentwood chairs that are synonymous with Irani cafés. The mirrored walls running the length of the room make you wonder about the various scenes and whispers they have contained, from political rallies during the independence movement, to the recent rumours in 2014 of the café's closing shutters, that left much of the city downcast in their wake. The century-old establishment has weathered the passage of time gracefully. The curtain call never came, and it reopened after a brief renovation. It remains a no-frills refuge for anyone looking for the staple *bun maska*, an Indian bun slathered generously with a dollop of fresh cream and butter, to be dipped into milky *masala chai*. The scrumptious *mawa* cake served at this establishment is truly a thing of legend, with early birds and night owls alike rushing to get their share from as early as 5AM. The buttery, fluffy, cardamom-infused cupcakes made with *mawa* (evaporated milk) often run out before 10AM, but other treats on offer include mawa puffs, mawa samosas, biscuits and walnut cakes. A somewhat grumpy, yet entirely reasonable, notice board hung towards the rear reads: "Cakes and biscuits once ordered will not be taken back." The faded allure of B Merwan & Co. endures in the fast-moving city, its name in bronze at the entrance welcoming you warmly, in a reassuringly firm font.

Words – AD | Photo – AA

Shop No. 1/ 2, Merwan Building, Frere Bridge, Allibhai Premji Road, Opp Grant Road Station East 400007 | 022 2309 3321 | No website

LEAPING WINDOWS CAFÉ

Located in the leafy, suburban neighbourhood of Versova, this café doubles as Mumbai's first comic book library, and it is nothing short of an escapist's haven. The quirky joint opened in 2012, inspired by Japanese comic cafés, and the décor — even at the canopied outdoor seating area — revolves solely around the universe of comic books, graphic novels and manga. Leaping Windows' divine house blend is a treat, including single-estate coffee from the hills of Coorg, as are the waffles. But down a small, spiral staircase in the corner of the room, inside the reading room, is where the magic really lies. Towering shelves stock a range of over 2,000 comic books, and the floor has been decked with cosy mats, cushions and bean bags. In the company of old comrades like Asterix, Tintin and Calvin & Hobbes, fans can also peruse the works of the modern masters: Alan Moore, Craig Thompson and Neil Gaiman, to name a few. *AD*

3 Corner View, Dr. Ashok Chopra Marg, Versova, Andheri West 400061

97699 98972 | leapingwindows.com

THE NUTCRACKER

The Nutcracker is strategically positioned opposite the One Forbes building, one of the largest office complexes in the area. It isn't particularly spacious, and on a typical weekday afternoon you might find groups of six or more squeezed around a table for four. As at most 'continental' establishments in India, the menu is a confusion of burgers, pastas, salads and panini – but the thing that sets it apart is that everything is cooked to perfection with a quintessential Nutcracker zest. One of the crowd favourites is the Seven Layer Cookie – a blend of biscuit crumble, Belgian chocolate, butterscotch and almond, served with a side of ice-cream. It isn't unusual to find people who've lunched or dined elsewhere heading over to The Nutcracker just for dessert. Regardless of what you eat or drink here, a visit will find you in one of the most stylish little cafés in the city. *AS*

Modern House, Dr VB Gandhi Marg, Fort 400023

022 2284 2430

thenutcracker.in

YAZDANI BAKERY

———

Yazdani is a wholly authentic representation of the Irani café, and one of the most charming little eateries Mumbai has hosted. Yazdani's name originates from the town of Yazd, which is the capital of the Yazd Province in Iran, and it is a hub of Iranian culture. This venue has been handed down through three generations and it is now more than six decades old. From the blue-green, peeling paint to the wooden benches and vintage posters of bodybuilders, Yazdani is a letter from simpler times. Most of these quaint establishments have vanished, making places like Yazdani even more precious. When here, the first thing you must have is the heavily buttered *broon pav*, a hard, crusty Irani bread, along with sweet tea. But other delicacies are not to be missed. The café is one of the few places in Mumbai that serve Iran's fiery ginger biscuits, while the *ladi pav*, a kind of soft bun, are some of the best available in both Mumbai and Goa. The Iranis and Parsis knew the art of leavening dough, but learned the technique of making panned bread from the Portuguese, who also taught them the use of hops in baking. The result is soft, delicious and keeps for days. Yazdani offers a varied and plentiful range of produce, from a seven-grain bread, and cheese and garlic buns, to Swiss rolls, chocolate bread, apple pies and freshly baked crumbly biscuits – enough to make you thankful that places like Yazdani have valiantly held on. *AA*

11/11-A Cawasji Patel Street, Fort 400001

022 2287 0739

No website

173

CAFÉ AT THE NCPA

TAJ MAHAL TEA HOUSE

Marine Drive is an exceptionally beautiful promenade, and adding to its grandeur is Nariman Point, situated at the end of the Drive. Here you will find the National Centre for the Performing Arts, or the NCPA, and nestled within its modernist architecture is a superb café. It overlooks the Arabian Sea, and enjoys almost unobstructed access to a constant, balmy sea breeze. Intended as a meeting place for people who come to enjoy the rich, cultural offerings of the National Centre, its menu predominantly features snacks and finger food. From burgers, sandwiches and milkshakes, to Asian food and crêpes, the café has something for everyone. Since it is run by Chef Farrokh Khambataa, who also runs the celebrated Asian restaurant, Joss, and the equally acclaimed Amadeus at the NCPA, it's unsurprising that the Asian and continental dishes are particularly good. *AS*

NCPA, Gate No. 2, Dorabaji Tata Road, Nariman Point 400021

022 6723 0110

ncpamumbai.com/restaurants

A small, sun-dappled patio welcomes you into this shaded space, that reveres not just the finest teas, but also the nuanced joys of the culture of tea-drinking. Nestled in the quaint neighbourhood of Bandra, this restored heritage bungalow retains the dreamy, transportive quality of the city's best hideaways. Wood-panelled ceilings and distressed beige walls lined with blue and white porcelain tiles, punctuated every so often with intricately-framed mirrors, wall art, or a few vintage kettles up on shelves, enclose three rooms separated by large archways. The furniture scattered across these is inviting, a motley collection of cane-webbed wooden chairs arranged around tables, stand-alone antique rocking chairs and plush armchairs tucked away in alcoves. Drinking chai has become an ubiquitous part of Bombay's culture, but Taj Mahal Tea House takes it up a notch with its flavour-filled offerings: from milky masala chais and infusions of black and green teas, to chai lattes, chai lemonades, and even chai smoothies. They serve house blends and handcrafted gourmet teas, as well as traditional Indian blends. The *tabla* (a Hindustani classical percussion instrument) that once belonged to the iconic tabla virtuoso Zakir Hussain, famous for his 'Wah Taj!' Brooke Bond Tea ads from the 90s, adorns a place of honour in one corner. As strains of classical Hindustani music weave unobtrusively through the hours, languid afternoons blend seamlessly into dusk through the sheer, white curtains, in the company of over a hundred books neatly arranged in various recesses. Titles by authors ranging from Toni Morrison to Urvashi Butalia beckon. With its air of elegance and warmth, Taj Mahal Tea House lets you choose your experience with every visit, whether it's a savoury High Tea Platter to which you'd like to treat yourself for brunch, or a blissful afternoon of daydreaming over a glass of saffron-infused Kashmiri *kahwa*. AD

36/A Sanatan Pereira Bungalow, St John Baptist Rd, General AK Vaidya Marg, Bandra West 400050

022 2642 0330 | tajmahaltea.com

EATERIES

लहान उपहारगृहे

TAJ ICE CREAMS

Situated in Bhendi Bazaar, in the Bohri Mohalla, Taj Ice Creams has a long and proud legacy of hand-churning its produce. Opening its shutters as Saraf Ali's Ice Cream in the late 1880s, this iconic yet nondescript parlour began its noble quest of bringing the working class the creamiest ices they could find, brimming with fruit and nuts. Despite changing its name to something snappier, the ice cream-making process remains the same over 125 years later, preserving the many of the methods of a time before electricity and cold storage were widely available. Boiled milk and fruits are poured into a copper canister, which is loaded into a wooden barrel filled with salt and ice, and then hand-cranked before being frozen at night and served fresh the next day. Some of the employees who churn the goods come from families who have worked here for decades, and it is run by fourth-generation proprietors, Abbas, Hatim and Yousuf, who have expanded Taj's repertoire to an impressive fifty flavours, though its seasonal mango and *sitaphal* (custard apple) variations continue to enjoy a special popularity. After navigating the pandemonium of the adjoining Mohammed Ali Road, or enjoying an aromatic meal at a *bara handi* eatery (where beef, mutton and curries are cooked in a mind-boggling series of twelve pots), freshly made dessert at this understated establishment is the only way to call it a night.

Words – AD | Photo – AA

R

Shop No. 7, 36 Khara Tank Road, Kumbharwada 400003

022 2346 1257

No website

SARVI

———

Located on the busy Nagpada Junction, opposite the Nagpada Police Station in Byculla, is Sarvi, an eatery without a signboard, whose kebabs are famous among the old-school connoisseurs of Mumbai. High ceilings, black-and-white chequered floors, peeling paint and circular tables characterise this corner restaurant in a district that was famous for the gangs it spawned, and the dons that began their reign here. Sarvi was also the haunt of Saadat Hasan Manto, one of Mumbai's most prolific chroniclers, and a man whose pen was filled with equal quantities of sarcasm, good humour and tragedy. Before you enter the venerable establishment, the smell of roasted meat hits you. Come here to savour the kebabs made from charcoal-grilled, fragrant mutton mince on skewers, served with bunches of fresh, green mint and chopped raw onions, along with a mint-and-raw-mango chutney. Other specialities include a preparation of goat or buffalo brains that involves scrambling them with a particular masala, called *bheja* (brain) *masala,* or bheja fry. A fatty dish served with a layer of oil floating on top, it is best enjoyed with warm, fragrant naan breads. Sarvi might seem nondescript and a little long in the tooth, but it is an authentic remnant of 70s and Bombay, and, for that alone, it is worth a visit. A word to the wise: while the food might be mildly spiced by Mumbaikars' standards, some of it might prove to be a little too hot for the uninitiated.

Words and photo – AA

RR

Dimtikar Road, Kazipura, Kamathipura 400008

098 2014 2967

No website

AMERICAN EXPRESS BAKERY

———

Kept in the family through the generations, this bakery's name was derived from the speedy delivery service it ran to the American cruise ships in the early part of the 20th century. Francesco Carvalho is the man behind an establishment that has weathered various storms over the years, from rationing in World War II, to the Emergency years of the 1970s, to the gentrification that's been spreading like wildfire in Bandra. For over a hundred years, sweet and savoury treats have been whipped up by the Carvalhos, whose first branch was located at Grant Road. Of the five outlets opened over the years, the one in Byculla, opened in 1935 in a wrought-iron building, and the cosy one on Hill Road, have best stood the test of time. 1950 saw Bertha Carvalho, the wife of the second-generation owner Joseph Carvalho, take the reins in a business dominated by men, and in an age when a working woman was an anomaly. She held the fort until her eldest son took over, thanks to which Bombay still has an array of mouthwatering treats for the soul on offer. Think assorted tea cakes, almond macaroons, puff rolls, plum cakes, tarts and Hungarian coffee cake, sitting pretty next to the Viennese truffles, cream rolls and the best, most wholesome cookies you're going to try in a long time. In case their overarching aims should ever be thrown into doubt, the company motto is clear: 'we knead your needs'.

RR

Multiple branches

americanexpressbakery.com

CAFE MADRAS

The need for Mumbai's millworkers and traders to have home-cooked meals not only made way for the *bhojanalayas* (North Indian-style eateries), but also brought about the rise of Udupi restaurants. Opened by a few enterprising families from South India, these restaurants focused on Tamilian and Udupi food for light breakfast meals, wholesome lunches and dinners, and local snacks. The food, which is mildly spiced, and usually made with fermented rice batter, is light, yet filling and healthy. It was no surprise that these Udupi establishments gained popularity, and soon they could be found in every nook and corner of Mumbai, dispensing their light, fluffy *idlis* and crisp, crunchy *dosas*, along with aromatic coconut chutney and sweet-and-sour *sambhar*, a watery lentil soup. Cafe Madras, located in the eastern part of Matunga, is one of the oldest establishments. When you step out of the cab, the first thing that hits you is the smell of coffee: Udupis were also famous for bringing *filter kaapi* or filter coffee to Mumbai. A cousin of the drip-brew method, South Indian filter coffee is robust, aromatic, medium-roasted, and blended with roasted chicory. It is served in two steel tumblers, one of which is wide-lipped and used to pour the coffee back and forth, thus bringing it to sipping temperature, whilst aerating it without the aid of a device such as the steam wand used for frothing cappuccinos. Still bearing a quaint, old signboard, Cafe Madras draws in large crowds, and there is usually a long line for lunch. Inside, the interiors are cool, and waiters bustle around on the marble floor, jotting down orders. From a fluffy semolina preparation called *upma*, to softer, pancake-like *uttapams* topped with onions, tomatoes and green chillies, or deep-fried *medu vadais* that look like savoury doughnuts, the list of things you can eat here is endless, and each meal has to end with a hot cup of filter kaapi. *AA*

RR

No. 38-B, Ground Floor, Kamakshi Building, Bhaudaji Road, Kings Circle, Matunga 400019

022 2401 4419 | No website

INDIGO DELI

_____

One of the pioneers of the 'deli experience' in India, and an extension of Indigo Restaurant, Indigo Deli is a chain of all-day cafés offering a combination of European and American comfort-food, coffees from around the world, a delectable selection of fresh breads and pastries and an impressive wine cellar. There are eight locations around Mumbai, each of which feature the signature muted décor of rich, earthy tones, plush leather and soft lighting. Indigo Deli is a modern example of Mumbai's successful assimilation of Western culture. Being the global, cosmopolitan city that it is, and a growing one at that, Mumbai continues to see a rise in eateries that borrow and replicate the dining experience from foreign countries, but few match the dexterity for which Indigo Deli has made itself famous. *AS*

RRR

Multiple branches

indigodeli.com

FRIENDS UNION JOSHI CLUB

_____

Many places in India have the tradition of the *bhojanalaya*, which literally translates as *bhojan* for 'food', and *alaya* for 'abode'. These are the 'abodes of food', or, as they are also popularly known, 'lunch homes'. If there's one thing you must know about Indians, it is that we love food, and we love feeding people. Be prepared for complete strangers to exhort you to eat till you're bursting at the seams, and still ply you with more food. At a bhojanalaya, the food is no-nonsense, yet delicious; it is inexpensive, yet well-made, with careful attention given to ingredients and flavours; it is not greasy; and, most importantly, there is a great deal of it, evoking the unmistakable taste of home. Since Mumbai is a city of migrants, there are lunch homes that specialise in cuisines from specific parts of India. Arranged like an old-school canteen, with seating on long tables and fans hanging from high ceilings, the Club is one of the city's best lunch homes, filling up with crowds of businessmen from the area during lunchtime on weekdays. Founded more than a hundred years ago, it was meant for the Gujarati men who left their villages to seek their fortune in Mumbai and missed home-cooked food. Located on the first floor of a structure that is probably as old as, or even older than, the notion of the lunch home itself, it is one of the best places for the Gujarati *thali.* Typically a thali is a very large stainless steel plate that is filled with four bowls of vegetable preparations, assorted flatbreads, two bowls of lentil preparations, buttermilk, poppadoms, pickles and dessert. At the Club, all of this is currently priced at Rs. 90, which is approximately £1. Think of it as the working man's filling, though no-frills, buffet. There are other places in Bombay that offer more rich and lavish versions of the thali, but if you want homemade authenticity, then places like the Friends Union Joshi Club are your best bet. *AA*

R

381-A, Narottam Wadi, 1st Floor, Kalbadevi Road 400002

022 2205 8089

No website

RESTAURANTS

रेस्टॉरंट

VERANDA

———

Tucked into a quiet lane off of Bandra's Linking Road, Veranda isn't a place you'd wander into idly. Like many of the city's hidden gems, it's a place that gets around through word-of-mouth. While Mumbai sees its fair share of new restaurant openings each week, very few manage to get it almost entirely right the from the outset. The interior is decked with large, eccentric pieces of décor, situated between traditional portraits and contemporary paintings. It has the essence of a *haveli*, or a rich ancestral home, but with a modern touch, a hint of the metropolitan curator, who is eager to embrace tradition while allowing for a casual, easy atmosphere that wouldn't be out of place on the other side of the world. The menu offers a contemporary twist on traditional Indian cuisine: each dish is plated per person, and presented in much the same way as many Western cuisines are. While the presentation might border on the experimental or conceptual, the taste is entirely truthful to its heritage – rich, unafraid to indulge in spice and, despite drawing on an equal blend of North and South Indian culinary influences, it is entirely authentic. The drinks menus are similarly expansive, with a delectable blend of easy cocktails.

Words – AS | Photo – AA

RRRR

331 Dr BR Ambedkar Road, Pali Pathar, Bandra West 400050

022 3312 6749

executiveenclave.com/Veranda.html

TRISHNA

———

In a city that is constantly growing, expanding, opening up its cultural borders, witnessing new experiments in the culinary sphere and attracting discerning palates from all over the world, it is heartening to find a few places that have stood the test of time. Trishna is one such establishment. Over fifty years old, it is an immediate gastronomical landmark for any resident of South Bombay, and an essential experience for all visitors to Mumbai. Kala Ghoda has seen a lot of growth over the years, but Trishna is still the most recognisable name in the area. Despite the creative, artsy, almost West-emulating aesthetic of many of the stores and restaurants that have recently come up in the area, Trishna stays true to its old-Bombay charm, with its plush sofa-style richly upholstered seats and gilded walls. When you order here, the neon blue fishtank that arrived at some point beyond memory gives a clue. The restaurant is best known for its seafood, which is cooked in the South Indian style, although it also offers a number of other Indian curries and naans. The garlic lobster is a perennial favourite. They're open for lunch and dinner every day, and are almost always packed, so don't forget to make a reservation.

Words – AS | Photo – AA

RRR

3/A Crystal Plaza, New Link Road, Andheri West, Azad Nagar 400053

022 3243 3631

trishna.co.in

BASTIAN

———

While Bombay boasts many traditional seafood restaurants that are worth visiting, Bastian shifts the focus from the overwhelming *masalas* (spices) in typical dishes to focus on the flavour of the seafood itself, with produce that's as fresh as it gets. The proprietor and chef, Kelvin Cheung, has become a hero in the city over the past few years, and a visit to Bastian – named for the friendly crustacean from Disney's The Little Mermaid – tells you why. Warm with wooden furniture and cosy seating areas – trendy-meets-ersatz perhaps best describes the décor – kitschy plastic crabs and other aquatic icons, including an almost life-sized alligator installation, reside on exposed brick walls that are dotted with porthole windows. There is a Polynesian-style tiki bar to boot. The restaurant gets most of its produce from the eastern shores of Chennai, and all its dishes are generous and masterfully-layered with flavours. Cheung brings together seafood cultures from Hong Kong to Hawaii, with the special 'seafood market' menu offering the choice between prawns, mud crab, lobster, the fish of the day or a vegetarian option, in one of six house sauces, at the time of writing. The sweet-and-sour Sichuan Snapper, and the Singapore-style chilli crab with its coconut-curry base, emerge as clear favourites among Bastian's denizens, while vegetarians swear by the wild mushroom *tom kha* made with market veg, including both King and Shimeji mushrooms. The standard menu is rich with promises of crispy and light *mantous* (Chinese buns, steamed or fried), and pillowy naan, as well as a few rice options. Mixologist Arijit Bose helped to set up the bar, so here as elsewhere, creativity abounds. *AD*

RRRR

B/1, New Kamal Building, Linking Road, Bandra West 400050

022 2642 0145

No website

ZIYA

_____

The Oberoi's website says that Ziya's Michelin-starred chef, Vineet Bhatia, has 'deconstructed and reinvented' Indian cuisine at this restaurant, and although that would be a difficult claim to verify, given that the definition of Indian cuisine might need to be as broad as the country that houses it, the food here is certainly delicious. It provides a uniquely modern take on 'Indian cuisine' in this city, if Michelin-style conventions of culinary-reconstruction are the type that appeal to you as a diner. Once fully on board, you will find Ziya to be great fun, if a little quiet, and the offerings, inspired by various regions and culinary traditions, to be visually and gastronomically satiating. *MS*

RRRRR

The Oberoi, Nariman Point 400021

022 6632 5757

oberoihotels.com/hotels-in-mumbai/restaurants/ziya

THE TABLE

_____

The concept of 'Global Cuisine' is desperately unfashionable in the West these days, but Mumbai doesn't really care about that. This restaurant is the winner of numerous awards, and takes an unashamedly fun approach to the food it serves. On the night of one of our visits, prawn dumplings appeared à la carte alongside tenderloin in red jus, while fish tacos were listed in the vicinity of Shimeji mushroom risotto and meatballs were served with French fries. If the curatorial approach causes you to skirt The Table, you're missing out. The quality of the food is exceptional, and, as dishes are served tapas-style, you can tailor your meal to create something a little more coherent and bespoke if you wish. The atmosphere is smart but the place buzzes, and you will find tables easy to come by at lunchtime, if not in the evening. It is also handily located a few steps from the Gateway of India. *MS*

RRRR

Ground floor, Kalapesi Trust Building, Apollo Bunder Marg, Colaba 400039

022 2282 5000 | thetable.in

PALI BHAVAN

———

Wooden deer heads, a black, white and green-chequered floor, ornate chandeliers, and wicker-backed chairs: Pali Bhavan offers the experience of an Indian nobleman's home from an era long past, where the doors were open to everyone and guests were filled till they could eat no more. Antiques sourced from around the country add to the carefully curated ambiance of the parlour of an opulent, although aging and sentimental *haveli,* or 'mansion'. The food has the appropriate richness and democratic spirit. Think of it as fine-dining-meets-street-food. While you peruse the menu, you are given a crisp, airy *puri* (a fried, puffed flour dumpling), accompanied by a vial of spicy water, an homage to Mumbai's ubiquitous street bite, the *paani puri.* Also on offer at the time of writing, to name a few dishes, are the *Mini Vada Pav* (a spicy mashed potato mixture, battered with gram flour, deep-fried and then put into a *pav* or a bun, very much like a slider) and the *Kaanda Bhaji* (slices of onion, mixed in batter along with various masalas and deep-fried), along with traditional Indian staples like *Paneer Tikka* (grilled cottage cheese) and *Kaali Daal* (pulses cooked in a rich, creamy gravy). Speciality dishes are available, like the *Galouti Kebab* (a tender mutton kebab). Pali Bhavan offers an experience that is at once both refined and deeply fulfilling. *AA*

RRR

10 Adarsh Nagar, Pali Naka, Bandra West 400050

022 2651 9400

No website

GALLOPS

———

Gallops is one of the appendages to the Royal Western India Turf Club. Situated inside a quiet building at the far end of the race track – past the finishing post and a distance away from the member's enclosure, amidst quiet green shade – it carries with it a certain Old World charm. The entrance itself is guarded by a formidable, heavy wooden door mounted with an iron crest in the design of an equestrian embellishment. The restaurant is a blend of fine dining with a certain 'club house' feel. The menu features continental dishes as well as rich North Indian fare, along with classic beverages. At the far end of the room there is a bar in the shape of a horseshoe. The detail in the décor is impressive, paying homage to the space's equestrian context, but in a way that is sleek, sophisticated, and perhaps a little tongue-in-cheek. Gallops has changed very little – if it all – since it first opened in the early 90s. A testament, possibly, to the unchanging nature of the Old World ideal, to which everything nostalgically alludes. *AS*

RRRR

Mahalaxmi Racecourse, Kharvi Road, Mahalakshmi Nagar 400049

022 2307 1448

No website

BARS

बार

INDIGO BAR & RESTAURANT

———

Coming up to the rooftop of Indigo Bar for the first time is a wonderful experience. There are other elevated drinking spots in the city, namely hotels that allow one to experience the expected views such as the sunset over the sea, but here the visitor is surrounded by something different. The colonial architecture that makes up the fabric of the residential district back from the Regal cinema, before one reaches the harbour, has been warmed and claimed by the residents of this wealthy set of streets. Old residences rise up around the tables and chairs that deck the roof terrace, which in turn is festooned with lights that cradle late-night drinkers. One might catch the odd glimpse into the windows of those that call this part of the city home, and the visitor from abroad might convince themselves during their time here that the city is indeed a familiar friend, wholly comfortable with their presence. The food is fine, and the rich colours of the interior entice, but if you really want to enjoy this carefully restored bungalow, grab a drink and head outside.

Words – MS | Photo – AA

RS Nimkar Marg, Grant Road East, Dalal Estate, Kamathipura 400008

093 2240 4801

foodindigo.com

YACHT

———

There are countless watering holes in the nooks and crannies of Bombay, but it's Yacht, a dive bar on Hill Road, right opposite St. Andrew's Church, that occupies a special place in its regulars' hearts (and, presumably, livers). Dingy and decades-old, Yacht is what is referred to as a 'quarter' bar, where the smallest alcohol order comes by the quarter bottle, making it the perfect place to retire at the end of a long day to nurse a cheap drink. An interesting assortment of patrons frequents Yacht, from broke college students and broke 'creative types', to the working class and working professionals. We'll be honest: Yacht is not for the faint-hearted or those who are easily offended. Its three rooms – two of which are air-conditioned – are pretty filthy, alternating between lighting which is seedy and dim, and lighting which is lurid and unnaturally white. The conversations have been known to turn heated at times, bordering on the aggressive, and there is the occasional rat to be found underfoot, hunted by the cat which otherwise prowls the tiled roof above. With its brusque waiters, no-nonsense food and rapid service, Yacht has become a bit of an iconic refuge from the snazzier, Drake-blasting pubs of fashionable Bandra, a place in which to set the world to rights until the last drink is gone.

Words – AD | Photo – AA

Near St. Andrews Church, Hill Rd, Bandra West 400050

022 2642 2718

No website

ONE STREET OVER

———

In recent years Mumbai was hit with the gastropub. Over here, the definition has been stretched to include edgier food and the kind of drinks you might expect to find in – well, a bar. Some even have mixologists, who are expected to whip up new and tantalising concoctions. They cater to pub-crawlers who are also well-travelled foodies. Simply decked out, with dim-lit, teal-and-mahogany interiors, One Street Over is helmed by the celebrated Canadian-Chinese chef, Kelvin Cheung – of Bastian fame – who is responsible for improving the fortunes of many restaurants in Mumbai. Cheung, along with his partner, Korean chef de cuisine, Boo Kwang Kim, brings a very personal touch to the menu. He has crafted it according to what he likes to eat when he is drinking or hungover, and so here you will find American comfort food with Korean influences. From hummus and burrata to Korean BBQ meats, and from chicken and waffles to cauliflower salad, the current menu is a mixture of healthy and moreish. Sometimes, Chef Cheung drops in after 11pm to whip up some late-night eats. The drinks, made by Arijit Bose,

a mixologist from Singapore, range from fruity and quirky to pleasingly potent. In one personal favourite, homemade grapefruit juice nestles with thyme syrup, Peruvian pisco and chocolate bitters. And for those who miss their malt, there's the Kelvinator, a mix of Jameson, Campari and sweet vermouth. Fun gastronomic experimentation, combined with a laid-back ambiance make One Street Over stand out in the Bombay gastropub scene. *AA*

Navarang Building, Ground Floor, 35th Road, Khar West 400050

022 2600 2224

No website

THE WHITE OWL BREWERY

———

The White Owl is the quirky result of Mumbai's newfound obsession with micro-breweries, brew-pubs and craft beer culture in general. A wise- and tribal-looking mascot adorns heavy glasses reminiscent of mason jars, and you can enjoy your beer while watching the brewing machines at work. Popular drafts include the Bumble, a honey blonde ale; Spark, a Belgian wheat beer; Shadow, an English Porter; Torpeda, a punchy American pale ale; Ace, a French cider. Seasonal specials are offered, such as Alfie, the mango ale. In fact, The White Owl now offers handy five-litre kegs, to take away, though these require a one-day liquor permit from the Excise Department. Happily, there is a kitchen with a carefully curated menu designed around the drinks to keep you onsite. *AA*

One Indiabulls Centre, Tower 2 Lobby, Senapati Bapat Marg, Lower Parel West 400013

022 2421 0231

whiteowl.in

IT HAPPENED IN NEW YORK

———

The nightlife of Bandra sees new bars and pubs opening up every month. It's easy to lose sight of new additions to the landscape, but It Happened In New York has succeeded in catching the attention of locals with the quality of its cocktails. The bar isn't so much a New York-style bar as it is an homage to the city itself. From the retro diner-inspired interiors to the New York Times-printed parchment paper popcorn sleeves, it has appropriated cultural references to the Big Apple in every element of its décor – as well as its menu. Hot dogs, bagels and cheesecakes are presented with a gourmet twist. The cocktail menu, which features classic favourites as well as the bar's own signature mixes, comes with added slices of trivia for those interested in learning about the drinks' origins, or the various avatars they've assumed over the years. *AS*

84 Chapel Rd, Sayed Wadi, Mount Mary, Bandra West 400050

022 2644 6161

No website

GHETTO

———

There are pockets of Bombay where the alternative rock scene of the 80s and the Grunge scene of the 90s are both still thriving, often side-by-side, and Ghetto is one of their most popular dens. The building that houses it seems to have withdrawn from the main road slightly, slouching back to brood away from the ongoing bedlam of Breach Candy traffic. A small wooden door leads into a modest bar and seating area, a space that has, since the mid-90s, witnessed the shenanigans of an Indian generation basking in the warmth of liberalisation. Distortion shreds the air as you enter, familiar guitar riffs greeting you like old friends and leading you into a larger room with two pool tables at the back. You're as likely to chance upon a Dire Straits tune as one by Nirvana here, and you will find yourself singing along with the rest of the bar as the evening progresses. The walls are covered with glowing graffiti and murals of music icons stand side-by-side with psychedelic one-eyed monsters. Words crawl around the images – scribbles and limericks from past patrons in various states of inebriation, with the witticisms ranging from the passable to the hilarious. For many who have grown up in Bombay, Ghetto is a nostalgic reminder of their hormonal, rock-fuelled teenage years. For every new visitor, it is a reminder that – of course – rock never dies. *AD*

30B Bhulabhai Desai Marg, Breach Candy, Mahalaxmi Temple, Opposite Tirupati Apartments 400026

022 2353 8418

No website

JANATA LUNCH HOME

The unassumingly named Janata Lunch Home at Pali Naka is often described on peer-review websites as 'Bandra's worst-kept secret'. Hidden in plain sight amidst a crowd of local establishments on one of the more bustling lanes of Pali Hill, the well-known Janata is a favourite among college students, young professionals and neighbourhood vendors alike. What appeals most to its eclectic clientele is its affordable and versatile menu, which encompasses everything from our beloved 'Indian Chinese' to sandwiches and samosas. It has a good range of beers, many imported. A television mounted on the far wall is almost exclusively tuned to a Bollywood music channel. There aren't a lot of places in Mumbai where you see people from all walks of life converging for a quick drink after a workday – but Janata is one of them. Its success may be, in part, a result of its affordability, but a certain amount of credit is due to its complete lack of ostentation, its satisfaction with itself as a distinctly local joint, and its refusal to cater to the current demands of customer service

trends. It is a place of nostalgia, a discrete focal point for a Mumbai that, though not disappearing, is dissipating, and that is only ever constant in places such as this. It is also a rarity in Bandra, in that drinks are served here late into the night, and they are available to take away along with the food.
AS

85 Gurunath Warda Marg, Nav Pada, Kurla West 400070

022 3312 6842

No website

Outer Limits
शहराची बाह्य हद्द

Photos –
Nirvair Singh Rai

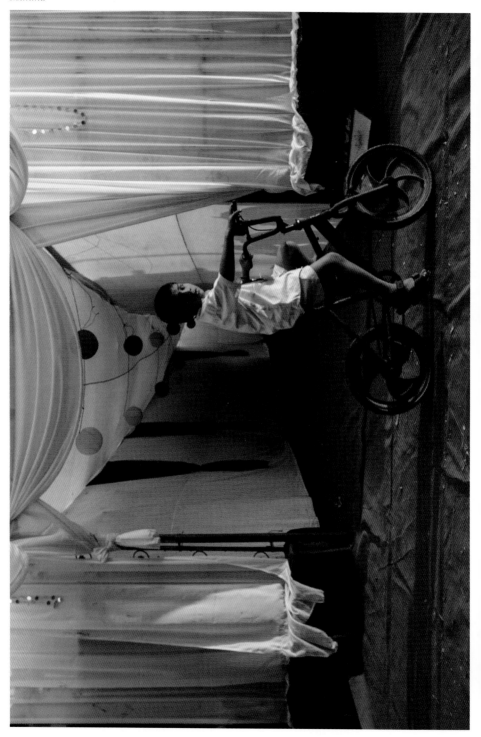

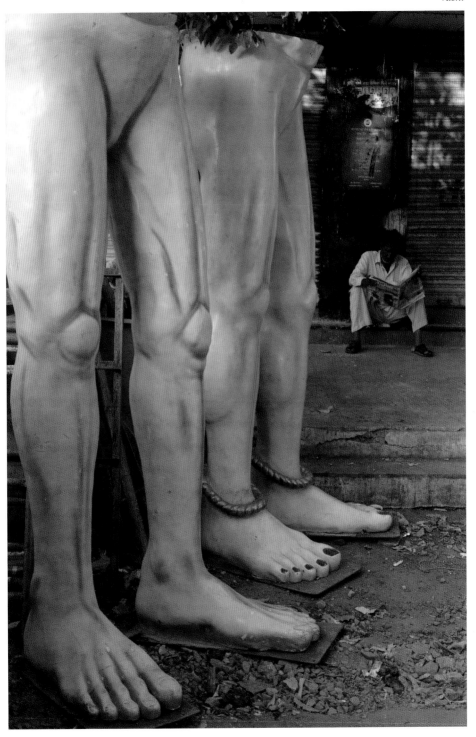

Home

घर

Words –
Avantika Shankar

Photos –
Matthew Smith

Dharavi

Bandra

Ａ city is only truly alive at night.

I first decided this for myself a few years ago, when I moved back to Mumbai after having studied abroad for four years. It was a strange sort of revelation I had, about the way the world interacts once the heat of the day dissipates. Brows no longer frown against the glare of the sun, and there are no appointments or deadlines keeping people on their toes. Cities slow down at night. Even cities like Mumbai, which never actually sleep, will slow down, and, for a moment or two, allow themselves to drift off into a dream.

It is in these moments, I think, that people, no longer shackled to their day jobs or their schools or their chores, find themselves able to do only what they mean to do, go to where they wish to go without urgency or the consequence of taking their own time.

When I say a city is truly alive at night, I think I mean 'alive' in the way that some might say only those people are who don't let the rules of society define them, who live on their own terms and who live in moments of absolute freedom and abandon. I think there is some truth to that definition of 'living', for people and for places.

Often on Friday nights, I walk with a friend in Bandra. Usually, it is just her and me. We've known each other since we were in school together, and we've stayed friends since, despite having gone to college in different countries. We have a regular Friday night routine: we have a few drinks at the Bandra Gymkhana – Old Monk with Coke – then we head for a walk on Carter Road.

The whole of Bandra seems to be out for a breather. It's barely eleven-thirty and most people's weekends have only just begun. There's the usual row of motorcycles parked by the footpath, with groups of teenagers wondering out loud where to head to next or why so-and-so isn't answering their phone. Most people end up staying there the whole night, by the sea, laughing, pretending to make plans for a more Instagrammable evening, but really quite happy just to be there.

It isn't just teenagers, either. Families are out, with young children overjoyed to be up past their usual bedtime. Old couples in gym shoes and track-pants sit on benches, their evening walks complete, looking passers-by up and down, saying nothing and saying everything. Milk vendors hang around the side of the road on their bicycles, selling Boost, a chocolate-flavoured drink, at twenty rupees a cup.

I walk with my friend and we aren't saying anything, lost in our own thoughts as two people usually are on a night like this. I look around and I think how different this place would be were this the early afternoon. Those cyclists and those rickshaw drivers would be caught in a roadblock, hurling obscenities at each other, one having cut the other off. Those teenagers would be rushing to after-school tuition classes, far more stressed-out than someone their age should be. Parents would be dragging their kids home – with errands to run and no time to stop and smell the metaphorical roses. No, those roses only bloom at midnight, when the obligations of the day are done – or, as tends to happen, they are put off till tomorrow. Right now, there is only sea and breeze. Right now is where we stand unshackled, unburdened by the commitments of our daily selves, with nowhere to rush to, and seemingly all the time in the world to stand and be as we wish.

I've lived in Mumbai all my life and I've seen it change drastically over the past two decades. I have seen quiet, unassuming alleyways get swept up by waves of gentrification; I've seen parks get turned into housing complexes. I have seen flyovers flooded during a manic monsoon downpour, seen highstreets alive and lit-up through the night during festivals, as crowded as if it were the middle of the afternoon, as loud as if there weren't a workplace to get to the next morning. I have seen the sunny days, the rainy days, the noisy days, the busy days. I've lived in this city my whole life and I know its pulse like I know that of my own heart.

Still, the only time I ever feel like I really know the city, that I really belong here, is in those moments late at night, looking out across the sea with strangers who, just like me, are, in that moment, exactly where they are meant to be.

In the day, the city is a machine; a machine in the sense that it doesn't stop. You could throw it under a flood or in the middle of a cyclone and the roads will still be full of people insistent on living their lives, getting where they need to be. I say machine because it functions without complaint or restriction, but I wonder whether to call it a machine is to imply that it is impersonal or inhuman, which couldn't be further from the truth. Everything in Mumbai is personal, everything is wrapped and packaged in layer upon layer of identity and history and heritage

Bandra

Bandra

Bandra

and culture. You are so much more than what you present to the world, yet everything you are is evident, almost immediately, to the eyes that watch you on the street, that recognise those slight mannerisms betraying the language you speak at home, or the shade of your skin that reveals which region you're from. People recognise these little bits of personality, because people take the time to notice, to pay attention.

I once got stuck crossing the street. It was a busy road going from the Haji Ali cross-section to the Tardeo cross-section. There were two signals at either end of the stretch but none where I planned to cross from. Like most people in Mumbai, I don't often bother looking for a crosswalk, and just dodge my way through to the other side. It's a skill that you develops over time and with practice, but you can still be caught off-guard in moments of chaos.

It happened to be rush hour on a weekday, and I had managed to cross one half of the road – the side where the traffic was going towards Haji Ali – but was left stuck in the middle. The road on the other side was impossibly busy, with traffic moving much too fast to dodge through. There doesn't happen to be a divider on that road, either, so I was just standing at an arbitrary point in the middle of a massively busy street, with traffic going both ways, hoping against hope that I didn't get my foot run over before I had a chance to get to the other side.

I don't remember how long I stood there, but it did seem like a very long time. I knew the traffic would eventually stop – it always did. There would eventually be a truck backing out of one of the buildings for which the traffic at the back would have to slow down, or there would be a taxi that would halt in the middle of the road, and allow its passenger to disembark at their leisure, oblivious to the honks and curses from the cars behind. Eventually, I kept telling myself, one of those moments of respite would come and I would run across the road. But the cars just went faster and the motorcycles closer and closer to my feet, and it seemed like it was going to take an eternity to get to the sidewalk, which was only about five metres away.

I had been seriously considering the possibility that this random, crowded road in Tardeo might end up being the place where I'd die when a woman in a pink sari – far shorter than I, rail-thin, veins and the contours of muscles lining her arms, wearing a pair of dark sunglasses that made her seem angrier than she probably was – grabbed hold of my hand and, shouting "Are you going to wait here all day?" in Marathi, dragged me across the street. Before I had the time to say thank you, she had neatly deposited me on the sidewalk and sauntered off.

I will never forget that, not least because I genuinely believe that woman saved my life, but also because it so perfectly encapsulates the nature of Mumbai. Mumbai is loud and scary and overwhelming – it's angry, rough, entirely surprising – but it is also kind. It is surprisingly warm, and comforting, in ways that are entirely unexpected.

There was another incident that really struck me. I was at the train station with my cousin – at Churchgate, to be precise – and it was about seven in the evening on a Friday, so it was packed. There were long lines for the ticket counter, and people were rushing to get to their train in time. As I walked past, I noticed that a dog happened to have fallen asleep in front of one of the counters, right in the middle of a line – and the line had actually curved around the sleeping dog. Rather than shooing the dog away, people simply lined up around it, giving it the space it needed to sleep. You hear stories about the cruelty that street dogs face on a daily basis, and about how so many other animals are abused around the country, whether it is for the sake of religion or out of pure spite. But then you also have instances like these. These are not overt shows of care and affection, but simple gestures of – literally – letting sleeping dogs lie: the compassion of sharing space, even when there isn't a lot to give.

And Mumbai knows a thing or two about sharing space. A local train on a weekday is probably the most accurate human re-enactment of a sardine can you could find. You will see trains pulling into stations with people hanging out of the doors to each compartment, and people on the platform still trying to push their way in. Even this would seem mad to an onlooker, but for the travellers there is still a method, even in the chaos.

When you get on a crowded train the other passengers will demand to know where you're going to be getting off. How many stops away your destination is, determines your position on the seat, or in line at the entrance if you happen to be standing. You also align yourself in such a way that you're facing the side of the train from which you'll be disembarking. There is a skill to the way in which people are able to manoeuvre around a crowded train – a skill that is absolutely dazzling to the untrained eye.

Vendors will hop from compartment to compartment, switching at each stop, selling everything from scarves and hair-ties to shoes and snacks and vegetables. The roads outside the the stations, too, are lined

Dharavi

Dharavi

Matunga

with fruit and vegetable stalls and street vendors. For many people who work late hours, this offers them a chance for some last minute grocery shopping.

I walk home from Dadar station most evenings. Dadar is possibly one of the busiest neighbourhoods in the city, likely on account of its being very centrally located. Two of the three train lines converge here, so the station is almost always crowded. I live very close to one of the city's best-known temples, Siddhivinayak Mandir, which is a Ganesha temple that serves as a point of pilgrimage for people across the country. Whenever there is a festival, however niche, the streets leading up to the temple will be vibrant with lights and music, pulsating Bollywood tracks interspersed with a few religious songs. Firecrackers burst with abandon on busy streets. Sometimes, two parades will cross each other side-by-side, neither one even remotely phased by the music of the other, the mismatched tunes and garbled rhythms doing nothing to stop the energy, the collective euphoria.

My grandmother tells me a story, sometimes, of when I was a baby. At the time, my family lived all together – my parents and grandparents, one aunt and one uncle, a dog and me – in a flat on the fifth floor of a building. We had a balcony that overlooked the main road that led up to the temple. I must have been about a year old at the time, because the story centres around the Ganesh Chathurthi festival, which happens around late August, and my birthday is in September.

My grandmother says there was a parade that day, and the whole family was out on the balcony to watch. I can imagine it wasn't much different than the parades that happen now: carriages drawn by horses decked in brightly-gilded blinkers, drummers and trumpeters, towering *murtis* (statues of figures from Indian culture) rolling down the streets on floats strewn with flowers, crowds of people dancing in the street, or standing on the sidewalk to cheer. Maybe there was less Bollywood techno music back then. Maybe fewer firecrackers, too. Certainly no Instagram. But the lights and the colours and the crowds and the noise will always be the same.

What happened that day was that I saw an elephant for the first time. He was part of the parade, garlanded and bejewelled, and was being led through the crowd, towering above it like the colossus he was. The one-year-old me was absolutely awestruck, and, long after the parade was over and the city had retreated into the quiet of the evening, I refused to leave the balcony. I wouldn't go to sleep that night because I was so excited, and I insisted on staying up to wait for it to come back.

I like this story because it says so much about India, and about people's relationships with it. So often, as a native, I tend to disregard visitors' comments about India being 'magical' and 'breathtaking' and 'exotic' and so on. Once you're used to a place, nothing really seems out of the ordinary. It amuses me, the way friends who are visiting will stop to take pictures of the cows on the streets, to which no local pays much attention at all, or the way they look in awe at the *chaiwallas* mixing tea on the street corners, pouring it between two tiny glasses held an arm's length apart with a precision that seems superhuman. These experiences have become so mundane to me that I dismiss them as things that are only attention-worthy to those from the West.

But the story of the elephant is special because it reminds me that, back when I was a baby and I had no understanding of culture or community, or what was normal or abnormal, back when I was small enough for everything and nothing to come as a shock, even back then, I was stunned into insomnia by the sight of an elephant in a parade. It is a story that captures the spectacle, the celebration and the complete, joyous abandon of Indian festivals.

I wonder now, too, whether the things that seem special to me are special only because they are so antithetical to that which I am used to everyday. Maybe I notice the quiet streets and the random, chanced-upon neighbourhoods that I come across so occasionally, merely because they are such aberrations in a city like Mumbai. What stands out to me, as a native, as someone who calls this place home, is very different from what draws in so many tourists from across the world.

Not many tourists come to Dadar. A lot of people who visit will go to South Bombay, because that's where the history is, the art and the museums. They then go to Bandra, because Bandra is where the young people are. It's where the new, experimental stores and cafés and bars are coming up, and it's close to the airport and the Bandra-Kurla business district. People will come to see the Siddhivinayak Temple, which is one of the biggest temples in the city – possibly among the most visited in the country, as a matter of fact – but not really for anything else. Dadar isn't a place I could easily explain to a siteseeing visitor. I find it hard to think of a specific reason for a visitor to come here. It's mainly residential, it's crowded beyond belief, it certainly isn't most people's idea of a relaxing day of fun. And yet, even to this day, I'm amazed by the things it has to offer.

Even on the days when there's a lull in the festivities and the nights are relatively quiet, there is a certain energy in the air that I don't often find in other parts of the city. In the evenings, street vendors will set up their *vada pav* (deep-fried potato and chutney with a bun) and *pav bhaaji* (fried vegetable curry with a bun) stalls, sending the heady smell of spices wafting through the evening. The shops at Dadar market glitter with rhinestone-studded dresses and sequinned tops and trousers – unapologetic in their flamboyance, undaunted in their appreciation of glamour. The boards at the front of shop doors feature posters of Indian and international celebrities from the early 90s, endorsing products I doubt they know they're endorsing, in haircuts and outfits that are probably never going to be in style again but which have wooed enough customers over the years to prove their worth. Popular eateries have people waiting hours in line at their doorstep, filtering out onto the street.

Further down the road from the market, the pace eases off. Owners will hang outside their stores, talking to passers-by – the sales of the day have been completed and the last customers have dwindled away, and now they'll take time to catch up with a neighbour. The mannequins that are placed out on the sidewalk during the day are brought back inside. People are packing up, on their way home, ready to retire for the evening.

I love Dadar for the exact reason that it is this tightly-packed tableau of city life. Everyone seems to know everyone, even though they don't. This is a tendency I most admire about my culture, this uncanny knack to appear familiar even with a complete stranger, to find a point of reference and forge an immediate kinship. Little children stand enthralled around a toy seller who demonstrates wind-up toy cars or squeaking bears or whatever the new thing happens to be that week. The parents gossip, pedestrians dodge through fruit-sellers on the pavement, couples sit on motorcycles chewing *paan* (herbs, spices and often tobacco, wrapped in a betel leaf), enjoying the last few minutes of a clandestine date.

The city exists in duality. It is often said, with regards to the economic disparity in the city, that this is a place where you can see extreme wealth standing side-by-side with extreme poverty. We see expensive products being bought and sold at stores that stand right next to slums, a Mercedes Benz driving next to a bullock cart. We're constantly reminded of the two ends of the economic spectrum, both of which exist simultaneously, everywhere.

And I think that there is another duality, too – a less tangible one. It's the duality of time. Mumbai of the daytime is hot and angry and flustered. It's the machine-Mumbai, a non-stop confusion of sight and sound and colour, a palpable monster blazing in the heat. And then there's the Mumbai of the night, a city whose pulse has softened, whose streets aren't swarming with commitments and appointments, but with people who are out to enjoy the breeze lilting in from the Arabian sea. There are people eating *chaat* (snacks originating in Uttar Pradesh) and *bhutta* (Indian corn on the cob), drinking *nariyal paani* (coconut water) and Thums Up, people out just to be out, to see their friends, to see the city wreathed in lights. This is the Mumbai that is most alive, to my mind – the city in which I, despite being a native, can still wander through as a tourist. It's a city unaffected by care or duty, in which those who have nothing to do and nowhere to be are not to be questioned. A city that is open, and vast, and continuous, and free, if only for a little while.

Overleaf - Dharavi